The Screenwriter Activist

The Screenwriter Activist
Writing Social Issue Movies

Marilyn Beker

Routledge
Taylor & Francis Group

NEW YORK AND LONDON

First published 2013
by Routledge
711 Third Avenue, New York, NY 10017

Simultaneously published in the UK
by Routledge
2 Park Square, Milton Park, Abingdon, Oxon OX14 4RN

Routledge is an imprint of the Taylor & Francis Group, an informa business

© 2013 Taylor & Francis

Library of Congress Cataloging in Publication Data
Beker, Marilyn.
   The screenwriter activist : writing social issue movies / Marilyn Beker.
      p. cm.
   Includes bibliographical references and index.
   1. Motion picture authorship—Social aspects.   2. Motion picture authorship—Political aspects.   I. Title.
   PN1996.B452 2012 2013
   809.2'3—dc23

                                                        2012003463

ISBN: 978-0-415-89714-3 (hbk)
ISBN: 978-0-415-89715-0 (pbk)
ISBN: 978-0-203-14578-4 (ebk)

Typeset in Caslon
by RefineCatch Limited, Bungay, Suffolk, UK

SUSTAINABLE FORESTRY INITIATIVE
Certified Sourcing
www.sfiprogram.org
SFI-00555
The SFI label applies to the text stock.

Printed and bound in the United States of America by
Walsworth Publishing Company, Marceline, MO.

For
P.Y. and GREG

Contents

Preface

My Reasons to Believe

I was born in a refugee camp. This is not immediately obvious. I'm a white woman of a certain age. I speak perfect un-accented English. I never talk about my early life. And yet, it's had a profound influence on my work. My parents are Holocaust survivors who wound up in one of the camps scattered throughout Europe to house those displaced, traumatized and nearly destroyed by World War II. My early childhood was filled with horrible, frightening, heart-breaking stories that made me want, even then, to be able in some way, to stop people from suffering. And I felt that I could do that because, mixed in with the tales of death and destruction, there were also stories about heroes who saved lives and did remarkable things. These heroes wore no capes or spangles. They were real people who overcame their own fears and inadequacies to accomplish what seemed impossible.

I took hope from these stories and people like my father who, because he didn't look Jewish, "bought" his Jewish friends from the Nazis. (They took the money, let his friends go and beat him to a pulp.) Or the Polish farmer Gnidula who hid my parents for 14 months in an underground bunker on his land and was shot for his refusal to reveal their whereabouts (you could say I'm here because of him). Or my mother's best friend Mala who after surviving the war, jumped in front of a mugger's bullet meant for her husband and was killed.

Stories like these, tucked in with the accounts of inhuman brutality, sustained me and gave me hope. I had to face the reality that the world could be a horrible place but it was also true that courage and self-sacrifice could trump that horror and ameliorate it. Heroes were real! People could make a difference! I clung to that and still do.

I believe in goodness, brotherhood and the ultimate nobility of humanity because I've seen, firsthand, evidence of those things in my own life and the lives of my parents and their friends. I've seen how "ordinary" people can do extraordinary things. The people my parents told me about and those I knew, made me realize that each one of us has the ability to, in some way, change lives (our own and others) by mustering our inner resources. If we cultivate and nurture those inner resources and truly change ourselves, we can indeed change our circumstances, our environment and yes, even the world. And we don't need guns or uniforms or money to do it.

In my case, I decided early on that since I had a talent for writing, I would use that as a "weapon" to end suffering in any way I could and I would motivate and encourage others to do the same. In my work as a writer and teacher, I've tried to help people understand that every life is filled with undreamed of possibilities, that words are powerful and can make a difference, and that possessing talent is a great responsibility not to be taken lightly. If those of us who've been given the gift of artistic acumen were to truly realize the impact that gift could have on a world desperate for meaning and purpose, we would all make a firm commitment to use our talent to ease suffering and turn darkness to light.

Acknowledgments

My teacher J. Oliver Black taught me the true meaning of success and for that and his generosity to me in all things I am profoundly grateful as I'm grateful to and for: my parents Joseph and Bronia Beker who taught me the meaning of nobility, justice and courage ; my husband Greg Rorabaugh whose love is a comfort and joy and constantly reminds me what's most important in life; my sister, Jeanne Beker whose energy, generosity, and style are truly amazing, my niece Bekky whose artistic sensibility and work to perfect it is exciting and exemplary, my niece Joey whose sweetness is translated into song; Sri Daya Mata who demonstrates courage and love, Bro. Anandamoy, Bro. Saralananda, Bro. Anhilananda whose wisdom and devotion are uplifting always, Br. Philip for his kindness, Karen Jones for her appreciation of my writing, Rosemary Massey for forty years of friendship, Carol and Richard Armour, who are greatly cherished and whose unswerving dedication and adherence to high ideals made the dream of community come true; John and Anne Pfluecke whose sincerity and love bolster that dream; Margie Friedman who's constant and true, the Ickowitz family (Ruth, Alan, Noah and Chana) who are very close, Hymie and Maggie Millstein, Ann Kindberg and Bob Nankin who make holidays bright; Teni Schwartz for her generosity and friendship at LMU, former students and now friends of whom I am very proud—Kelly O'Hara,

Vanessa Coto, Jason Endres and Darris Gringeri—ethical people who live their high principles; Irene and Juliette Gringeri who are dear and special, Professor Jay Doughtery for his legal expertise, Johnathan King, Susannah Grant and Eilis Kirwan for their time and world-changing work, my editors at Routledge Linda Bathgate and then Erica Wetter who saw the merits of this book's subject and championed it, Jeffrey Davis for his encouragement and support, Loyola Marymount University for providing an environment where social issues are important and Paramahansa Yogananda for everything!

INTRODUCTION

What's It All About?

All artists have opinions about life and society and create their work specifically to express that opinion. That's why all artistic work has a point of view and it's usually the point of view of the artist who has something she thinks is necessary to say. Every work of art exposes directly or indirectly, the artist's sensibility and world view. Screenwriters are no exception.

That's because, at its core, every screenplay is "about" something and has a theme and sensibility that drives it. This "about" is deeper than the surface story. It's the ultimate message of the movie—its essential theme and sensibility. The more aware the screenwriter is of what that essential theme and sensibility is, the more that writer is in control of the screenplay and the more that writer can manipulate the characters and events to get a specific reaction from audiences. In this case, manipulation is a good thing. All screenwriters want audiences in the palms of their hands and work mightily at their craft to achieve that result. Screenwriters who write social issue screenplays are particularly interested in captivating audiences and stirring up their passion by inspiring them to get involved in the issue at hand.

This book is for the screenwriter who believes that movies can make a difference in people's lives and motivate them to take action. It's for screenwriters who are compassionate and who ardently believe in good stories centered around people taking a stand, often against great odds. It's a book for screenwriters who know that heroes aren't always those with the biggest muscles or magical powers and who realize that sometimes just enduring can be heroic. And ultimately it's for screenwriters who one day want to look back on the movies they've written and feel good about themselves because, while entertaining audiences, they've also been able to teach them something and encourage social activism that has meaning and substance.

Activism can take many forms. It doesn't have to be political or partisan although it does have to take a stand. That means that this book does not encourage either a liberal or conservative point of view. It does, however, encourage self-examination, social awareness and an understanding of what it means to be engaged in the human condition. Most screenwriters would like to think that any movie demonstrates these things. This book, however, emphasizes how social issue movies in particular, exalt these things and use them to affect societal change.

What's a Social Issue?

A social issue is a topic that influences, or has an impact on, a large number of people. These issues tend to be sweeping and broad but social issue movies make them more real by focusing on their effects on specific individuals or groups of individuals. For example, divorce is a huge social issue that affects millions of people but a good social issue movie (as we'll see later in the book) brings this issue home by demonstrating its effect on one family or individual. Social issue movies make social issues real, personal, dynamic and relate-able to audiences by getting them involved both emotionally and intellectually.

This book demonstrates how to do that using a series of topics to consider while preparing for and writing social issue screenplays.

The Steps to Writing a Social Issue Movie

Motivation

We'll begin with a look at what inspires people to become engaged with social issues in the first place. To do that we'll draw on the words and experiences of world leaders and great thinkers who have determined that it is important to get involved in social causes for the greater good.

Taking Action

We'll encourage you to recognize how the power of words can make a difference, how films have influenced culture and how individuals and groups of individuals have made a social difference. We'll introduce a definitive list of social issues and demonstrate that social issue movies can be successful by listing all the Academy Award winners through the years that have had social issue themes. Just because you're writing a social issue movie doesn't mean that you've got to be dull, preachy or "small." Social issue movies can be bold, expensive, spectacular and mainstream. It all depends on how you present the material and what kind of writer you are. While it's true that many social issue movies have a small indie feel, there are just as many (think *Avatar* and *Juno*) that have a commercial mainstream appeal.

Inspiration

Personal introspection is important. Writers need to draw their stories and characters from personal experiences and knowledge. It's the writer's job to make emotions and reactions, conflict and tension visual, to make the audience relate to the characters in a very personal way. Audiences can recognize when writers are faking it. That means that you need to be able to relate to the emotion you are expressing and that means that you also need to relate to the social issue in some special way. We'll explore that as a way of choosing the social issue your movie will be about.

Character

Characters are incredibly important in social issue movies because they take the issue to the audience. You'll need to choose characters that are strong, yet vulnerable and who have the ability to move your story forward. This means that you'll have to establish both a back story and a pretty complete character biography that includes an examination of how each character reacts and expresses him or herself emotionally. We'll introduce a template to help with that.

On the Shoulders of Giants

Now that you have your social issue and have chosen characters, we'll demonstrate, through specific examples, how characters are used to drive the social issue. Through these examples, you'll see how a character's innate characteristics are used to engage with the specific issue and make it relatable to audiences.

True or False?

You may have decided to write a true story based on a real person. We'll consider the role of embellishment and exaggeration, your responsibility for accuracy, and also your commitment to the issue and the "real" person. We'll also discuss the acquisition of rights and some legal steps you'll need to take to protect yourself and your project.

Plan of Attack

Once you've figured out your issue, your story and your characters, you'll have to decide how you want to write your screenplay. There are lots of ways to do this. To make things easier, you'll be presented with an *outline template* (**Outline Magic**) that will help you outline your story with perfect adherence to structure. Then, you'll be given *seven social issue screenplay models*. Each model will be defined and analyzed via the outline template, to see how social issues are brought forward to coincide with screenplay structure and to create audience interest.

Research

Research can give you your story if you don't yet have one or change the story you do have. This step demonstrates how, but will also show you how not to get stuck in research quicksand. Lots of writers use research as an excuse to delay writing. You'll be convinced that you can start writing with a minimum of research and do the heavy lifting as you go.

Getting it Made

All screenplays are hard to sell and social issue screenplays are no exception. Social issue screenplays have a little edge because of their nature. You'll learn how to take advantage of that edge and look at some strategies that have been successful and some that haven't. The 2010 movie *The Whistleblower* will serve as a useful case study in beating the odds.

Afterglow

A reflection on what keeps us writing and committed.

Spoiler Alert!

I couldn't help it! In using movies as examples, I've had to give away plots, describe characters and divulge endings. I know it's a terrible thing to do so before you read this book, you might want to watch these movies or, you can (particularly in the section on screenplay models) watch the movie as you follow along with the analysis. Here's my list:

It's a Wonderful Life
Sullivan's Travels
Norma Rae
Philadelphia
Good Morning Vietnam
Million Dollar Baby
Vera Drake
Casablanca
Erin Brockovich
The China Syndrome
Silkwood
Wag the Dog
A Few Good Men
A Beautiful Mind
The Squid and the Whale

The King's Speech
Hotel Rwanda
Juno
The Whistleblower

1

MOTIVATION

Words to Write By

When John Lennon told us we all want to change the world, he was right. We all want to make our mark in some way. Each one of us wants our existence to count for something meaningful. Of course, as Frank Capra pointed out in his 1946 film *It's a Wonderful Life*, each one of us does change the world just by being in it. In that movie, the James Stewart character (George Bailey), wishing he had never been born, is suicidal until Clarence (an angel) shows him how the community would have fared had he never existed. Just like George Bailey, each of us, just by being born, has altered the future.

Imagine what the lives of your family, friends, neighbors, and community would be like if you had never lived. If you take the time to do that, you'll probably see that you have made a considerable difference, and usually, for the better. But sometimes, making an "unintentional" difference for the better isn't enough. There are those of us who believe that it's incumbent upon each person to actively try to improve the world in some way. Each one of us can fight in the ongoing war against oppression, evil, hatred, discrimination, injustice and inhumanity and we can do it in ways that don't involve spending a lot of money, getting beaten up, or taking a bullet. Even small actions taken with great heart can contribute much.

We are inspired by the words of people who've made a difference. Their quotes could fill books but here are just a few of them:

> **Paramahansa Yogananda:** "Seek to do brave and lovely things that are left undone by the majority of people. Give gifts of love and peace to

those whom others pass by . . . As the vital rays of the sun nurture all, so must you spread the rays of hope in the hearts of the poor and forsaken, kindle courage in the hearts of the despondent and light a new strength in the hearts of those who think they are failures."[1]

Robert F. Kennedy: ". . . each of us can work to change a small portion of events, and in the total of all those acts will be written the history of this generation. . . . It is from numberless diverse acts of courage and belief that human history is shaped. Each time a man stands up for an ideal, or acts to improve the lot of others, or strikes out against injustice, he sends forth a tiny ripple of hope, and crossing each other from a million different centers of energy and daring those ripples build a current which can sweep down the mightiest walls of oppression and resistance."[2]

Mother Teresa: "In these times of development, everybody is in a hurry and everybody is in a rush and on the way there are people falling down who are not able to compete. These are the ones we want to love, serve and take care of . . .

We ourselves feel that what we are doing is just a drop in the ocean. But if that drop was not in the ocean, I think the ocean will be less because of that missing drop."[3]

Bishop Desmond Tutu: "So often when people hear about the suffering in our world, they feel guilty but rarely does guilt actually motivate action like empathy or compassion. Guilt paralyzes and causes us to deny and avoid what is making us feel guilty. The goal is to replace our guilt with generosity. We all have a natural desire to help and to care and we simply need to allow ourselves to give from our love without self-reproach. We each must do what we can."[4]

Dr. Martin Luther King, Jr.: "When an individual is no longer a true participant, when he no longer feels a sense of responsibility to his society, the content of democracy is emptied."[5]

"It really boils down to this—that all life is inter-related. We are all caught in an inescapable network of mutuality, tied in a single garment of destiny. Whatever affects one directly, affects all indirectly. We are made to live together because of the inter-related structure of reality."[6]

"Every man must decide whether he will walk in the light of creative altruism or the darkness of destructive selfishness. This is the judgment. Life's most persistent and urgent question is, "What are you doing for others?"[7]

The Dalai Lama: "We need to base our lives on altruistic concern aimed not just at our own private welfare but also at the good of society."[8]

"Each one of us is responsible for all humankind. We need to think of each other as true sisters and brothers and to be concerned with each other's welfare. We must seek to lessen the suffering of others."[9]

Bill Gates: "Not everyone can go in the field, or even donate. But every one of us can be an advocate for people whose voices are often not heard. I encourage everyone to get involved in working for solutions to the challenges those people face. It will draw you in for life."[10]

Karen Armstrong: "Compassion doesn't mean feeling sorry for people . . . it's not pity. We are putting ourselves in other people's shoes to feel/ experience with the other. Realize we have an absolute responsibility to end the suffering of the world, to feel responsible for our peers and to try to alleviate suffering all around the globe. This is our duty as human beings."[11]

St. Francis of Assisi: "Lord, make me an instrument of thy peace. Where there is hatred, let me sow love; where there is injury, pardon; where there is doubt, faith; where there is despair, hope; where there is sadness, joy; where there is darkness, light."[12]

Swami Sri Yukteswar Giri: "Those who remove our troubles, dispel our doubts, and bestow peace are true teachers. They perform a Godlike work. Their opposites (those who increase our doubts and difficulties) are harmful to us and should be avoided like poison."[13]

Exercise

Find a quote that motivates you, write it down and keep it beside your computer as you write. When the writing becomes difficult or you doubt yourself and your work, read it over to keep you going.

2
Taking Action

Lots of us have taken inspirational words to heart. We give money, we work in soup kitchens, we tutor, we join the Peace Corps, we help friends and neighbors in difficulty. Americans are among the most generous people in the world. We came to the aid of victims of the Japanese and Haitian earthquakes, the Indonesian tsunami, the Darfur tragedy and more.

A Tradition of Good Works

According to *Giving USA*, a report compiled annually by the American Association of Fundraising Counsel, Americans gave more than $307.75 billion to their favorite causes despite the economic conditions in 2009. Seventy-five percent of that amount came from individuals. But it's not all about money. Many of us give our time and energy too.

The Corporation for National and Community service said that in 2009, 63.4 million Americans volunteered to help their communities by distributing food, working in education, health, civic services, sports, the arts and religious organizations. In fact, 35.6 percent of volunteering was based in religious organizations. It's after all the fundamental teaching of all religions to serve and give. The Bible is often quoted as encouragement to tithe—particularly the book of Malachi (the last book in the Old Testament):

> *Bring all the tithes into the storehouse and there may be meat in my house, and*
> *prove me now herewith saith the Lord of hosts, if I will not open you the*

windows of heaven and pour you out a blessing, that there shall not be room enough to receive it.[1]

Hence the saying, "he who gives, gets."

All Christians are urged to tithe 10 percent of their incomes. The Q'uran urges all Muslims to give to charity. The Torah requires all Jews to tithe as well. Buddhists are enjoined to practice compassion. But even atheists, taking humanism for their creed, can and do join the giving in the belief that, as a species, we need each other to survive and by helping each other, we can all make a contribution toward world betterment. As Sri Daya Mata says, "the once vast world is now more like a household, with each member interlinked and dependent on the others."[2] Screenwriters are in a particularly advantageous position to make a significant contribution to world betterment. The films we write affect large international audiences and by writing movies about social issues we can inspire masses of people to take action that could truly change the world. That's because all the movies that screenwriters write have a definite effect on mass consciousness. Every 35-foot image projected before an audience influences that audience in some way. Media theorists have written scads of books explaining just how films influence both our culture and our psyches. I won't belabor their points. Everyone now knows that the images movie audiences see have an emotional effect which can cause specific actions. Movie images can incite audiences to buy products, dress in specific ways and even go to war.

The Influence of Movies on Trends and Fashion

Advertisers know this and push for "product placement" in films to up sales of their products. (Product placement "involves incorporating brands in movies in return for money or for some promotional or other considerations."[3]) As an article in the *Journal of Marketing* reports, "product placement spending in the U.S. grew at an annual rate of almost 34% to $2.9 billion in 2007 and was projected to reach $5.6 billion in 2010."[4]

Morgan Spurlock's 2011 feature documentary *The Greatest Movie Ever Sold* is specifically about product placement—a behind the scenes look at how advertisers operate in today's movie market. Spurlock (who made *Super-Size Me*—the 2004 movie about the fast food industry) entirely financed his film by advertising and product placement.

Fashion Designers know that movies set fashion trends. Regular folks, not necessarily into style, still want to look like characters in their favorite films. In the silent era all the girls in America imitated Louise Brooks' bobbed hair. In the 1930s and 1940s, women wore pants like Katharine Hepburn, high heels like Joan Crawford and long locks like Veronica Lake. In the 1950s, they wore skin-tight dresses like Marilyn Monroe and pearls like Audrey Hepburn. James Dean made white tee-shirts popular when he wore them in *Rebel Without a Cause*. In the Sixties, *Bonnie and Clyde* had women wearing berets and guys wearing vests. *Easy Rider* mainstreamed hippie chic. In the 1970s *Saturday Night Fever* had every guy wearing a white suit (just like John Travolta) to his prom. *Annie Hall* made women dress Diane Keaton-like in over-sized men's wear, hats and ties. In the 1980s *Flashdance* was responsible for main-streaming workout wear—leg warmers and off-the-shoulder sweat shirts, *Out of Africa* made safari-wear standard and *Wall Street* got every guy a pair of suspenders. In the 1990s, *Reservoir Dogs* made black suits and skinny ties popular, *Pulp Fiction* glamorized white shirts and black pants. *The Matrix* got people into long black coats. In the 2000s *The Devil Wears Prada* made tall boots a come-back trend and *Sex in the City* made every woman crave Manolo Blahnik shoes.

All Art is Propaganda

These days everything is moving so fast—going from screen to shop at warp speed and vice-versa—that the relationship between film and fashion has become almost symbiotic and simultaneous, both influencing the other. In lightning bursts, street and screen have collided to forge new lifestyle patterns and even new ways of thinking. People are more comfortable about alternative realities (*The Matrix*, *The Truman Show*, *Inception*, *The Adjustment Bureau*). The line between "reality" and science fiction is blurring precisely because of modern technological breakthroughs. People are more inclined to support scientific advancements and alternative philosophies because of what they've seen on screen.

Governments have known this for a long time and have taken advantage of film's power to make audiences amenable to political positions, particularly concerning war. In World War II both sides used movies. Hitler and Goebels made a point of using films to tout their evil Nazi cause and spread racism. America and its allies used films to appeal to people's sense of righteous goodness and humanistic values in the face of this evil and racism. It worked. While Germans bought into negative Nazi propaganda about the Master Race, turning a blind eye to the horrors of the "Jewish Solution," Americans bought into the positive propaganda of patriotism, personal sacrifice, liberation and universal freedom.

Propaganda has become somewhat of a negative word—it is perceived as a technique of dogmatic coercion but, in fact, propaganda is simply a neutral technique as defined by any standard dictionary as "the systematic propagation of a doctrine or cause or of information reflecting the views and interests of those advocating such a doctrine or cause."[5] Propaganda can, and has been used to do good.

When all World War II American films (musicals to mush) encouraged audiences to buy war bonds, sales skyrocketed. According to U.S. History.com in 2010, more than 85 million people (more than what was then half the population of the US) bought $185.7 billion worth of bonds—a record that's never been broken—and helped America win that war.

In those days, there was nothing subtle about getting Americans to join the war effort. The social issue messages in films made during World War II were blatant. Characters portrayed by big time stars told people exactly how to behave and think in wartime. In *Casablanca* (1943—winner best screenplay) Humphrey Bogart stood on a rain slicked runway and talked about personal sacrifice.

RICK

I've got a job to do too. Where I'm going, you can't
follow. What I've got to do, you can't be any part of,
Elsa. I'm no good at being noble, but it doesn't take
much to see that the problems of three little people
don't amount to a hill of beans in this crazy world . . .

In *Mrs. Miniver* (1942—winner best screenplay) the vicar gives a speech about public commitment to the war, in a bombed out church:

VICAR

We, in this quiet corner of England, have suffered the loss of friends very dear to us. . . . . . And why? . . . . . I shall tell you why. Because this is not only a war of soldiers in uniform. It is a war of the people, of *all* the people, and it must be fought not only on the battlefield, but in the cities and in the villages, in the factories and in the farms, in the home and in the heart of every man, woman and child who loves freedom! Well, we have buried our dead, but we shall not forget them. Instead they will inspire us with an unbreakable determination to free ourselves and those who come after us from the tyranny and terror that threaten to strike us down. This is the people's war! It is our war! We are the fighters! Fight it then! Fight it with all that is in us, and may God defend the right!

Now, because audiences are more sophisticated, social issue sentiments have to be expressed less didactically—with elegance and subtlety— but can still pack a punch if the emotional sub-text is there. Take a look at this exchange from *The Hurt Locker* (2009—winner best screenplay).

SERGEANT JT SANBORN

I'm ready to die, James.

STAFF SERGEANT WILLIAM JAMES

Well, you're not gonna die out here bro.

SANBORN

Another two inches, shrapnel zings by; slices my throat—I bleed out like a pig in the sand. Nobody'll give a shit. I mean my parents—they care—but they don't count, man. Who else? I don't even have a son.

JAMES

Well, you're gonna have plenty of time for that amigo.

SANBORN

Naw man. I'm done. I want a son. I want a little
boy, Will. I mean, how do you do it, you know?
Take the risk?

JAMES

I don't know. I guess I don't think about it.

SANBORN

But you realize every time you suit up, every time we
go out, it's life or death. You roll the dice and you deal
with it. You recognize that don't you?

JAMES

Yea . . . Yea, I do. But I don't know why. (Sighs) I
don't Know, JT. You know why I'm that way?

SANBORN

No. I don't.

These men are fighting in a different kind of war and so there are no
patriotic speeches about right and country. These men are just doing a
job and the statements about their ambiguity are subtle. No one is
saying "Why are we in this?" or "I don't care about this war and the
people in our country don't either." Conversely, they aren't saying
"We're here to do a job and do it right because people depend on us,
because we are liberators, because we believe in peace and freedom
for all mankind." The audience is left to form its own conclusion. No
one needs to spew out a message. And yet the unspoken message is
clear—the men are confused, disheartened and uncertain about why
they do what they do. This is also an interesting piece of propaganda
trying to sway audiences. Recognizing the power of propaganda
and its true definition, George Orwell intimated (as the title of one

of his books of collected essays says) that all art is propaganda since it puts forward the philosophy and viewpoint of the artist. The degree to which the audience buys into it depends on the artist's skill. Orwell said

> Propaganda in some form or other lurks in every book, . . . every work of art has a meaning and a purpose—a political, social and religious purpose—our aesthetic judgments are always colored by our prejudices and beliefs.[6]

Orwell is right. In my first book, *Screenwriting with a conscience*, I make the case that every film is "really about" something—that every film has a message of some kind.

> As writers we all must ultimately face the truth that the story is only a chiffon scarf over the rippling bosom of its message . . . all movies say something even if the person who wrote them is conscious of that or not. And all movies make a strong statement, even if that statement is silly, inconsequential or just plain dumb (party until you throw up for no good reason; boff your brains out for no good reason; shoot, kill, maim for no good reason). It's because I believe that images are powerful, meaningful and mighty things, that I also believe that the people who create them on such a large scale (a 35-foot idea is hard to ignore) have a responsibility as part of the human family to wield their power wisely.[7]

In that book I go on to make the case for writing ethically—that screenwriters should remain true to their "messages" no matter what. Since I wrote that, I've seen how writers looking to define their messages slowly come to the realization that maybe a dumb, inconsequential or silly statement at the root of the movies they write, isn't satisfying enough. Screenwriters who have developed a conscience usually come to realize that they'd like to influence audiences in good ways—ways that could make a distinct difference, ways that could impact and change lives for the better. I see screenwriters with consciences beginning to have a greater interest in writing about social issues.

However, they aren't interested in writing documentaries which are entirely reality based and tend to have more specific and smaller audiences. Instead, believing that narrative films can do more than documentaries to get a foothold in the collective consciousness of general audiences, ethical screenwriters want to write narrative films showcasing social issues in artistic and dramatic ways.

What are these "social issues?" They are things which have an effect on society and those dwelling within it often on a profoundly personal level. Issues can be the result of legislation or of personal behavior. They are far-reaching and affect a great many people. The following is a list of the most basic and obvious social issues.

Keep in mind that these issues can be complicated and bifurcated. They can include extremely compelling sub-issues which can also stand alone. For example, the corporate greed issue can extend into the homelessness issue (caused by foreclosures) and even into environmental and public health issues (caused by industrial pollution such as oil and toxic spills); immigration issues can extend into labor issues (such as sweat shops). You may find yourself writing about two or three issues at once under an umbrella issue that contains subsidiary social issues.

The Social Issue List

Abortion
  Teen pregnancy
  Adoption
Addiction
  Smoking
  Drugs
  Alcohol
  Sex
  Gambling
Animal rights and protection
Abuse of power
  by politicians
  by the media
  by military
Breakdown of the family
  Divorce
  Single parent issues

Criminal justice
   Capital punishment
   Violence
   Gun control
   Police corruption and brutality
Censorship
   Political repression
Child abuse
   Can include human trafficking
Civil rights
Corporate greed
Disabilities
   Physical, mental
Domestic abuse
Education
   Illiteracy issues
The environment
Euthanasia
Genocide
Gay issues
   Marriage and adoption
   Discrimination
Human rights
   Includes torture
Homelessness
Hunger
Immigration
   Refugee issues
Labor practices
Mental health issues
Native rights
Peace issues
   Nuclear disarmament
Political corruption
Poverty
Public health issues
   Health care
   Chemical and/or biological contamination

Racism and discrimination
Sexual harassment
Suicide
War issues
Women's rights

Screenwriters who are passionate about these issues believe, as Tolstoy said,

> Love for humankind won't let us serve it by making our work consist of amusing the well-fed, while leaving the cold and hungry to die of want.[8]

However, even the most altruistic screenwriters eventually must realize that no matter how committed they are to their causes, their first responsibility is to entertain. The media activist Herbert Marcuse admits that "even the most radical art can not in its denunciation of the evils of society dispense with the element of entertainment."[9]

Unfortunately, most altruistic screenwriters get so caught up in the social issue they're writing about that their screenplays become preachy, boring, heavy handed or maudlin. Without the entertainment factor, audiences will be turned off and stay away in droves. That would have a drastic effect on the social issue the screenwriter wants to put forward and ultimately for the screenwriter who, based on bad box-office, may never work again.

Successful professional screenwriters who write about social issues make sure their films are entertaining. When screenwriters entertain, and at the same time deliver, social issue messages that strive to prevent "the cold and hungry" from "dying of want" they achieve the remarkable.

This isn't a new concept. Consider the 1941 Preston Sturges film *Sullivan's Travels*. In that movie a director, determined to make a social issue film called "Oh Brother Where Art Thou?" rides the rails to identify with and research the downtrodden man. The director discovers at the end of the movie, that what really benefits society is not necessarily a dour exposé about horrid conditions but something that makes people laugh, entertains them and takes them out of themselves. The movie he made still made audiences aware of the plight of the downtrodden man but wound up being incredibly entertaining. (The Coen Brothers' 2000 comedy *Oh Brother Where Art Thou?* was a riff on Steven's gem and won them an Oscar.)

Entertainment combined with message is paramount, but entertainment doesn't always mean using comedy. Social issues also make great dramatic stories because they are based on humanistic concerns that involve compelling characters who go through gut-wrenching, heart-tugging, heart-warming, tragic and interesting situations that involve audiences emotionally. *When compelling characters come up against a social issue that creates tension, challenges them, forces them to act or reflect, that movie becomes entertaining and incredibly successful!* (We'll explore the importance of character in social issues films later.)

Consider the social issue movies that have won Oscars for best picture and/or best screenplay (original or adapted) and earned dazzling box office receipts as well:

Social Issue Oscar Winners

1942	Casablanca—War issues
1942	Mrs. Miniver—War issues
1945	The Lost Weekend—Addiction (Alcohol)
1946	The Best Years of Our Lives—War issues
1947	Gentleman's Agreement—Racism and discrimination (religious discrimination)
1954	On the Waterfront—Labor practices
1957	Bridge on the River Kwai—Bravery in war
1958	The Defiant Ones—Racism and discrimination
1961	Judgment at Nuremberg—Genocide
1962	To Kill a Mockingbird—Racism and discrimination and criminal justice issues
1967	Guess Who's Coming to Dinner—Racism and discrimination issues
1967	In the Heat of the Night—Racism and discrimination issues
1970	M.A.S.H.—War issues
1975	One Flew Over the Cuckoo's Nest—Mental health issues
1976	Network—Corporate greed and abuse of power by media issues

1976   All the President's Men—Political corruption
1977   Julia—Genocide
1978   Coming Home—War issues
1979   Kramer vs. Kramer—Breakdown of the family (divorce)
1980   Ordinary People—Suicide
1982   Missing—Political corruption
1982   Gandhi—Peace issues (non-violence)
1988   Rain Man—Mental health issues
1991   Thelma and Louise—Women's issues
1993   Schindler's List—Genocide
1994   Forrest Gump—Mental health issues
1997   Good Will Hunting—Education issues
1998   Gods and Monsters—Gay issues
1999   Cider House Rules—Abortion
2001   A Beautiful Mind—Mental health issues
2002   The Pianist—Genocide
2004   Million Dollar Baby—Euthanasia
2005   Brokeback Mountain—Gay issues
2005   Crash—Racism and discrimination issues
2007   Juno—Abortion and teen pregnancy
2008   Milk—Gay issues
2008   Slumdog Millionaire—Poverty
2009   The Hurt Locker—War issues
2009   Precious—Child abuse
2010   The King's Speech—Disabilities

And these are only the issue-oriented films that have won Oscars. There are many many more social issue films you might be able to name that did very well.

Participant Media—*The* Social Issue Production Company

Social issue films are big business. Participant Media for example, is a production company based in Los Angeles, entirely committed to social issue films. It has made many social issue documentaries: *Waiting for Superman* (2010—Education), *Countdown to Zero* (2010—(Nuclear) war issues), *The Cove* (2009—The environment re ecological crime), *Food Inc.* (2008—Public health issues re food safety), and the multi-award winning *An Inconvenient Truth* (2006—The environment re climate change) but it has also created narrative social issue movies.

With films like *The Help* in 2011 (Civil rights issues and labor practice issues), *The Informant* in 2009 (Corporate greed re multi-national price fixing), *The Soloist* in 2009 (homelessness and mental health issues), *Charlie Wilson's War* in 2007 (War issues re land mines), *The Kite Runner* in 2007 (War issues), *The Visitor* in 2007 (Immigration), *Syriana* in 2005 (Political corruption and corporate greed), *American Gun* in 2005 (Criminal justice issues re gun control and violence), Participant media has not only greatly increased world awareness of specific and compelling issues but has also prospered and serves as a beacon for writers and audiences who believe in social issue narrative movies.

Participant's founder and Chairman is Jeff Skoll, a philanthropist and social entrepreneur. Participant's website tells us that Skoll was the first full-time employee and first President of eBay. He developed eBay's inaugural business plan and led its successful initial public offering. eBay has since become the world's largest on-line marketplace.

After pioneering the creation of the eBay Foundation through the allocation of pre-IPO shares, Mr. Skoll founded the Skoll Foundation in 1999 to invest in, connect, and celebrate social entrepreneurs and innovators dedicated to solving the world's most pressing problems. Skoll founded Participant Media in 2004 with, as the website says, "the belief that a story well told has the power to inspire and compel social change." Participant's films are accompanied by social action and advocacy campaigns to engage people on the issues addressed in the films.

The company says it seeks to entertain audiences first, then to invite them to participate in making a difference. To facilitate this, Participant creates specific social action campaigns for each film designed to give a voice to social issues that resonate in the films. Participant teams with social sector organizations, non-profits and corporations who can, with Participant, offer specific ways for audience members to get involved. These ways include action kits, screening programs, educational curricula and classes, house parties, seminars, panels and other activities and are ongoing "legacy" programs that are updated and revised to continue beyond the film's domestic and international theatrical, DVD and television windows. To date, Participant says it has developed active, working relationships with 600 non-profits which collectively have the potential of reaching over 75 million people.

Jonathan King is the executive vice president of production for Participant. He oversees development and production of the company's narrative feature films. I spoke with him in November of 2011. "People have always made movies that deal with social issues ever since movies were invented," he said. "Social issues are the subject matter of movies because they are the subject matter of life all around us and they are dramatic stories or inspiring stories or funny or sad and the only thing different about Participant is that we make those kinds of movies exclusively. The idea behind Participant is that once you've got people's attention and their passion you channel it into real action."

As an example, King used *The Help*. "We asked ourselves, 'How do we want to empower people with this movie?' That movie is so much about people who had no voice that finding a way to use their voice to change their circumstances is inherent in the material. So we partnered with storytelling groups. The Moth (a New York City based non-profit organization that conducts live storytelling events) was a big partner for us. We developed a whole campaign to do with school kids and we said, here's a forum, here's what these women did in this movie. They told their stories and in that changed their circumstances. What's your story? That's what The Moth exists to do—to facilitate storytelling—so we said let's partner with this organization that already does something we want. We didn't want to invent their program. We wanted to funnel people into it and make it complementary to our movie."

Participant does sometimes invent programs or produce events. For instance, when the company went to Cannes with *Fair Game* (the 2010 political corruption issue film in which CIA operative Valerie Plame discovers her identity is allegedly leaked by the government as payback for an op-ed article her husband wrote criticizing the Bush administration) Participant held big panel discussions and a media day about that issue. "Ongoing projects, however," said King, "are taken on by those with whom we partner."

But staging events and having non-profits help promote your cause is expensive. King says that the money for doing that is the cost of promoting Skoll's vision. "Sometimes it's paid out of the marketing budget of the movie. It's not really movie marketing but it's cause marketing so if you get people to care about your movie they are going to show up to the movie. The distributor who is all about making money is in favor of that if it drives people to the movie."

Participant is not a distributor. It's a financier and a production house that also generates movies internally about issues it cares about. "In 2012 for instance," King said, "we are going to be shooting a movie set in Colombia about industrial exploitation in the developing world. We were wanting to make a movie about that because you are constantly reading about some accident or some toxic spill that happens and the company will cover it up and get off easy.

"One of the driving questions that plagues me in the middle of every night is how do you compete with every other movie that's out there, so we said ok we want to make a movie about industrial exploitation in the developing world and we're going to ask people to pay for it. What can we do to make it entertaining? In reading all the news account of the tragedies that happen , we found some version of this sentence that comes out whenever some journalist writes those kinds of stories : 'this ground is haunted by the victims of this tragedy'. What if that were literally true? What if we made a ghost story about that? So our development team took that idea and wrote a paragraph and we pitched this out to see if any writers wanted to come out and write something on it. We heard pitches on the core of that idea and then hired writers who pitched us a really compelling story that was grounded in reality but had a ghost story around it. It generated from the issue. But the story/issue has to be authentic. In any movie, authenticity is really important. We can make a ghost story but if you can't peel the onion back and say that at the center of this story is a real issue and this really happens and that is really the way it happens, if there isn't a core of reality then it isn't really a movie for us."

King says that most of Participant's projects are incoming but if the company can't find what it wants, it will "build it." "We are a small company," says King. "There are three of us working on narrative and one part-time guy in London. *The Help* came to us. On something like our movie in Colombia we couldn't find the movie we wanted to do so we had to build it. *Contagion* (the 2011 thriller about the outbreak of a deadly disease) was sort of a hybrid. That movie came out of *The Informant* (the 2009 film about price-fixing based on evidence by a delusional whistleblower)."

"There's a scene in *The Informant* where the Matt Damon character is on the phone, the Scott Bakula character is standing next to him. Scott sneezes and Matt's internal monologue is 'oh great now I'm going to get sick and I'm going to give it to. . . .' Out of that Scott Z. Burns (the screenwriter) and Steven Soderbergh (the director) said let's make that movie and we paid Scott to write the script. He did tons and tons of research everywhere and we built that. All the research and reality is great, but if Scott hadn't written a really compelling involving story about those people, it wouldn't be a movie."

Contagion is an obvious social issue movie (about public health issues) but what about movies where the social issue isn't that prominent? King uses the film *The Best Exotic Marigold Hotel* which came out early in 2012 as an example. "It's about a bunch of British retirees who for a variety of reasons are priced out of their retirement in London. They can't afford the housing they want. They can't afford proper health care. All these different issues that are real issues for seniors. The characters in the movie separately respond to an ad for a luxury retirement hotel in India. And then they get there and it's not at all what they thought it would be and romance and comedy and adventure ensue.

"People can look at that movie and think it's a wonderful movie with Maggie Smith, Judi Dench, Bill Nighy, Tom Wilkinson—all the sirs and dames—and you can just look at that and say that's a wonderful movie, but what it sets in motion is real issues that all of us who are getting older or who have parents who are getting older are dealing with. So the issue is in there. But that wasn't what that movie was built on. I'm not sure if we said let's make a movie about seniors that we would build that one but it came in and was such a wonderful script we said it was perfect because that's a way of talking about these issues without being depressing or morbid. It's a movie that has to compete with every other movie on a Friday night."

"We never know where we're going to find what we need. We take an expansive view. There could be an issue in anything. It's a big decision to take on a movie and say this issue is important enough to us that we're going to deploy the resources of this company behind it. That's not set in stone and it's a different conversation every day."

But Participant does have its pet issues and they are linked with Skoll's Global Threats Fund—an organization whose primary purchase is to focus on five main social issues: climate change, water scarcity, pandemics, nuclear proliferation and Middle-East conflict. "These things are really threatening our existence on the planet as a species," says King, "and if we're not developing something or have something addressing those then I have to find something. I feel that for now we've made what would be considered the definitive movie about a virus pandemic (*Contagion*) so we're not going to do that again next year. We'll figure out different ways to keep that issue going."

"We're developing something about the Mid-East conflict—a new way to think about that, a couple of things about water and nukes—those are the global threats and we have to focus on that. And if something comes in or if there's something we think is important and we care about (like the exploitation of emerging economy) we'll build something about that. It's fluid and unique to this company."

King isn't the only one in the company who is committed to social issue movies. He says that "everyone who works at Participant works here because of the company's mission. They are motivated by the mission of the company. I make movies and I want to compete with every other commercial movie but I also care about this stuff. Most people who work here are social or political minded."

How successful has Participant been in changing the world? "Some of it is measurable and some of it is not," says King. "*Contagion* created a lot of awareness about the threat of virus pandemics and about what our government is doing and should be doing and should be doing more of to prevent and manage virus outbreaks throughout the world. But that awareness is not measurable. When an editorial appears on the *New York Times* op-ed page referencing the movies you can speculate on how many people read that and how many people will do anything about that. There's sometimes when you can say this happens specifically because this happens. When the documentary *The Cove* (exposing shocking dolphin abuse) came out in 2009, there was text at its end telling you what to do if you wanted to stop the dolphin slaughter and you know how many millions of people did that and you know that it stopped. It's easier with documentaries."

"Take *The Visitor* (a 2007 film about illegal immigration) for example. Participant is represented by a law firm and every law firm has to do pro bono work so with that law firm we helped to create a program to train lawyers to help deportees who did not have any representation. So if you see the movie and at the end of the movie it says go to Take Part/*The Visitor* one of the things you can do if you're an attorney and you need pro bono hours is to be trained to represent a detainee. Our law firm does the training. Thousand of lawyers did that. That became a measurable program."

"There was a moment around this time last year when The Food Safety Act and New Start were trying to get through congress. *Food Inc.* (a 2008 documentary about the corporate-controlled food industry) was used as a tool to convince legislators to pass this thing and it happened. What percentage of influence did that have? Immeasurable. But did it help? Yes. *Countdown to Zero* (the 2010 documentary about nuclear proliferation) was given a secret private screening at the CIA. Secretary Clinton watched the movie on her plane and there was a lot of pressure exerted on congress to pass New Start. Did we help? Yeah. Can you measure it? No, but we know it happened. How many people paid money to see *Countdown to Zero*? Not very many unfortunately, but if you can make a feature film to educate people who aren't legislators about the issue and it's a hit movie, then great, that's just another piece of the mosaic."

"We don't want to often tackle a thing where we feel there is nothing we can do about it. But that's our challenge to say that even though the issue feels overwhelming, here's what you the viewer can do and communicating that to audiences is our primary mission. But it still has to be a movie. People aren't going to be motivated by something unless you've made them cry. At the risk of sounding glib, unless it's going to make me laugh, scream or cry, why will I pay for it? It's not a right to have your movie in the theater. It's a privilege and you've got to fight for it. You've got to fight for everybody's money. People have a lot of choices."

Screenwriters have lots of choices too. The bumper sticker is "so many social issues, so little time."

How can you choose an issue to write a screenplay about? The following exercise will help you do that.

Exercise: Issue Selection

1. From the list in the chapter above, pick out those issues that "speak" to you.
2. For each, write down what about it is interesting to you, what moves you emotionally about it and why you think it's socially important.

   Keep in mind that the issues themselves are *neutral*. You can be either for or against an issue. During this exercise, it's important to NOT be swayed by political correctness. Be honest and write down exactly what you think about the issue.

   The issues that moved you most and on which you had definite opinions are the ones on which you should concentrate.

In the next section, we'll delve deeper into why you chose the issues you did and how you can work them to your advantage in a screenplay.

3
INSPIRATION

At the beginning of this book I told you about my history because I want to make the point that all of us are in disguise. Each one of us has emerged from a private past of which the world is entirely unaware. But this past is essential, especially for a writer because it's from this past that she draws much of her material. The exigencies of life provide the writer with the subtext and fabric of her work. Sometimes, the writer is unaware of how that happens. Interests and preoccupations seem to bubble up out of nowhere. The reality is that they bubble up out of experience and reaction to events that make deep grooves in the subconscious mind.

In my case for example, my refugee experience has made me particularly sensitive to the plight of refugees all over the world. It has also made me sensitive to the horrors of war and profoundly interested in peace and non-violence issues. In addition, my parents' experience as Holocaust survivors has made me passionate about the issues of discrimination, civil rights, and world hunger. My own experience as an immigrant has made me interested in immigration issues.

Each one of these issues strikes a very real emotional chord in me and, through analysis, I can trace the source of that chord to a visceral moment of personal experience that led to definite actions.

I marched for the rights of blacks to vote in Selma, Alabama, demonstrated against the brutality of the police at the Democratic Convention of 1968 in Chicago, protested against the violence at Kent State. Even as a teenager, that emotional chord drove me to try and make a difference. For me, writing about social issues was natural. I'd spent so much of my youth thinking about injustices and ways of solving them that it made sense that I should, when I had the opportunity, use my talents to try to remedy these injustices. As a newspaper reporter, I investigated stories about disenfranchised people forced from their homes because of corporate development. As a radio "personality" and writer I wrote and read radio stories about the experiences of immigrant children. As a magazine writer, I wrote stories about people fighting to maintain and express their own cultures through their art and, as a consultant in the Arctic, worked with Inuit and Dene to help them make films about their own threatened cultures. As a screenwriter, my first short narrative films were about racial tensions in public schools and as a documentary film maker I pursued issues of women's rights and inner city women resisting gang involvement. My feature films tend to be about strong women who persevere against all odds and even though I tend to write screwball comedies, they make serious points about life. My stand-up, television and radio comedy did too. The same is true both for the novels I'm writing now and for my academic books.

Your life might not have prodded you to think in this direction when you were a kid, but it's not too late to do so now.

Issue Mapping Exercise

I believe that each writer who champions an issue has something in her background, even though she may be unaware of it, that makes her able to relate personally to that issue. Of course some issues are more at the forefront than others. That's why serious introspection is essential to discover why a certain issue speaks to you. When you find that out and are able to make an emotional connection to it with something in your own life, you'll be able to work from a point of passion and involvement that will energize your social issue screenplay. Your ability to make a personal connection with an issue will make you more likely to create characters that can engage the issue in such a way as to make audiences emotionally involved. The way to do that is to create an *issue map* of your personal life.

1. Look at the issues you chose in the last exercise.
2. For each issue, since screenwriters are visual people, conjure up an image that directly relates to it in your own life. For

example, in my own life, my first issue (human rights) conjures up an image/memory of barbed wire and crowds of people in the refugee camp where I lived for the first few years of my life. I remember no privacy and lots of noise. This was one of my earliest images.

For the issue of hunger, my image/memory is of sailing to Canada on a converted troop ship and eating the whites from the back of orange peels because I was so hungry and there was nothing else to eat. By bringing to the fore these images, you should be able to see how I've developed an emotional connection to each one of them. You need to do that for yourself to create your personal issue map addressing when you first became aware of the issue in your life and what incidents sparked this awareness.

Now include the characters you became involved with at the point in your life when the issue first came to your attention. Among my characters are the woman who took care of me in the refugee camp after her own children died in the war, the man who jumped off a moving boxcar to fetch my ball while we were being transported to the troop ship; the woman who laughed and forgave me when I threw a roll in which she'd hidden a precious gold coin, from a high window into the street to feed what I thought was a hungry dog. When an image/memory is linked with a character, it tends to become even more powerful.

At the end of the exercise, rank the issues that have emerged. While doing this exercise, most likely you will discover that your issues tend to lump together. You may even whittle down your list to fewer issues than you initially thought interested you. The issue that has the highest ranking is likely the issue you are most passionate about at the moment and one on which you'll base your screenplay. This doesn't mean that you'll never write about the other issues. You may do so in the future, but at the moment—in this place and time, the issue at the top of your list speaks most loudly to you and so you should make it the subject of your screenplay.

As the story develops, you can do the research to flush out the outline and even write the first draft while you're researching. Remember, the characters, their reactions and relate-ability are more important than exposition. Obviously you want audiences to understand the issue so information is necessary, but you also want them to connect emotionally to your characters in their struggles with the issue. The more subtle the exposition and the more compelling the character, the better the issue comes across. Find the emotional backbone and the compelling tension of your story before you flush out the expository details!

4

CHARACTER

Characters give social issue movies their depth, their punch, their memorability. Social issue screenplays are propelled by characters. As I've already said, facts and events by themselves are neutral. Their impact lies in the effect they have on people. Plot develops as a result of how characters experience and react to events and facts. Because of this, you need to create/choose characters that are strong, interesting and complex enough to take on your issue because in their actions and reactions you'll unfold your story, put the issue forward and make the audience understand and relate to that issue.

In addition, keep in mind that to get a name actor interested in your project, it will be necessary to create a character with depth, range and passion. Having a name actor eager to appear in your project is a sure way to get it made. To help you visualize your main character, you could even write that character with a famous actor in mind. But, while you can use this technique to help you, you shouldn't so specifically tailor your project to the "name" that your movie can't be done without that person. Make sure that your main character isn't a "star" but a real person that a star can inhabit the way that Susan Sarandon inhabited Sister Helen Prejean in *Dead Man Walking*, or the way that Sally Field inhabited Norma Rae in *Norma Rae*. Visualizing a famous name to help define the character is a good way of keeping on point, but be sure to make your character "real" enough so that any good actor could step into the role. After all, good actors are chameleons and should be able to become any character.

Thinking of an actor or not, the first thing you need to do is develop a complete character biography for each of your main characters.

These biographies will help you understand thoroughly how your characters relate to the social issues. To do this, you will need to repeat the Issue Mapping exercise you performed earlier, only this time, you will need to morph your own issue map into an issue map/character biography for your main character(s). You can include images and events that took place in the characters' lives well before the beginning of the movie. You may never use these images or the events you conjure when you write your movie, but they will inform you about what shaped the characters and make you understand them on a very deep level. In this way, as you propel them through your screenplay, you will be able to make their actions and reactions believable and solid because those actions and reactions will be based on history.

Lots of writers I've worked with tell me they don't like writing character biographies. They think it's busy work and a chore that bores them. But in the process of writing their scripts, they come to realize that their initial ideas about biographies were nonsense. They come to find out that without knowing their characters intimately, their screenplays fall flat and usually end up plot heavy and substance light.

Since every piece of dialogue comes directly out of character and every action can be explained by character, it's essential to create a biography that is vital, complete and informative. I always recommend writing the biography in a story format. A point form biography answering "essential" character questions (e.g. hair color, education, family background etc.) isn't rich enough to give writers the nuances necessary to create a character with subtext and substance.

Let's look at an issue map biography for characters we plan to use in a script about native rights. The story we might want to tell is one in which a Native Rights Activist discovers that politically charged government action is about to destroy her people's cultural heritage. This story might be inspired by an actual event (historical or current) or by an imagined incident that could play up the danger of community extinction.

I chose native rights as an example because of my own issue map. I first learned a lot about native rights and history when I was researching my Master's thesis on Pauline Johnson, a native Canadian poet who wrote extensively about native culture at the turn of the last century. At that time, the Master's program I attended demanded courses plus an extensive thesis to be defended verbally before a committee (much like a PhD thesis). Because of this, I spent lots of time learning about the pressures put upon indigenous people as they tried to move forward in white society.

Years later, I worked in Canada's Arctic with Inuit and Native Canadian film makers teaching them to make films about their own cultures. The Canadian Government established television in the Arctic and programmed typical "southern" shows (e.g. Hawaii Five-O) to blast into indigenous homes. After a few years, the Inuit and Dene realized their cultures were being eroded. Their children stopped speaking their native languages and refused to learn the old skills—hunting, fishing etc.—essential to sustain life. Violence increased and many teenagers began to demonstrate disassociative behavior, when previously they were very community oriented. To articulate the problem and to try and solve it, I spent time on reservations and in small remote native communities—some of them only accessible by air. During that time, I became intimately involved with native culture and native activism and learned a great deal about native rights and social issues surrounding them. I've been passionate about native issues ever since.

That's why, drawing from my personal issue map, I chose native rights as an example and again, drawing from the people I met during the Arctic Project (#3 of the Issue Mapping Exercise) I'd create a character biography of my main character (a native American rights activist) starting this way.

Issue Map/Biography of Main Character Angela— A Native American Rights Activist

"The first Indian Angela saw was in an old cowboy movie. She was eight when, sitting on the worn red velvet seats of a run-down revival neighborhood movie theater, she rooted for the men in white hats hoping they'd shoot a pile of Indians before the lights went up. Two years later her life changed. Her mother died and she discovered that her biological father (someone her mother never mentioned) was a Native American living on a reservation three states away. Because she had no other living relatives, the state got her father to agree to take her. The summer she moved there, Angela found out all about

Indians. Her knowledge made her ashamed of herself and her early ignorance."

From there, I would describe her learning curve through significant incidents and images and again using powerful images, describe her relationships on the res. Finally, I would write about how she became sensitive to native issues through more incidents and images and how that sensitivity turned her into the native rights organizer she is at the start of my movie.

When you are writing your own issue maps/character biographies, be sure to include several strong images (as you did in your own issue mapping exercise) to "pin" your character emotionally to the issue at hand.

To better define that emotional connection, you also need to create *emotional biographies* of your main characters. Following is a template you might use to do that. I've filled in the template using my native rights movie as an example.

Angela's Emotional Biography

SORROW/GRIEF

Angela was ten when her mother died. When that happened, she was devastated and swore she would never allow herself to feel that kind of sorrow again. She shoved her feelings deep down inside her, so much so that she has trouble feeling sadness about anything and certainly she never expresses it. Instead, she uses sarcasm, wit, humor or just plain detachment to counteract any feelings of sorrow that might creep in. (I can use this character trait in my screenplay when I'm writing dialogue and to demonstrate her interaction with people she meets for the first time.)

JOY

Angela likes to have a good time. She felt alienated and different growing up but found that when she was happy, people liked her so she spends lots of time clowning around, being funny or just plain exuberant. People think of her as a jolly person who laughs easily and is always in a good mood. (I can use this in my screenplay when Angela tries to fit in to new situations.)

ANGER/RAGE

Angela is still very angry that her mother never told her anything about her biological father. She's also angry that he "disappeared" shortly after she was born and never tried to contact her. She used to fantasize about having a father to protect her when neighborhood bullies used to taunt her and she resented the fact that she had no male role model and nobody to bring extra money into the house so her mother wouldn't have to work so hard. She developed a seething rage that she kept at bay. Now it comes out suddenly, in awkward moments, and sometimes in spite of herself. (I can use this in the screenplay to draw out and perhaps resolve her relationship with her father.)

FEAR

Angela fears abandonment. She fears being alone. That's why she always surrounds herself with people and keeps busy. She'll do any-thing to be a part of things. (I can use this in my story when she's pressured to give in to the prevailing and powerful pressure groups.)

LOVE

Angela craves love. Because of that she's a people-pleaser but deep down she hates being so malleable and ultimately winds up hating the people she's trying to please. Angela has always craved pets because they would give her something to love, but her mother has always warned her that pets would die and break her heart. That's why Angela loves animals but is afraid to get close to them just as she's afraid to get close to people. (I can use this in my screenplay to create a love relationship she could develop with another activist.)

FRUSTRATION

Angela has trouble with languages and isn't detail or craft oriented. When she gets frustrated with tasks, she simply gives up and walks away. She hates spending time practicing things she doesn't pick up right away. (I can use this in scenes where Angela is challenged by her tribe's elders for not knowing her Native language and skills.)

HOPE

Angela has always had high hopes. Encouraged by her mother to be better than everyone else, she hopes one day to become a writer and a public figure but she doesn't know how she'll achieve these goals. She spends her time keeping a journal and one day plans to write a book. (I can use this in my story to show how Angela is articulate and can negotiate public forums.)

GREED

Angela has always despised greed. Her mother taught her to share and she always grew angry when she saw others keeping things for themselves. Angela has a tendency to be overly generous. She gives away much of what she possesses. This feeds into her need for acceptance, certainly, but also emphasizes her belief that no one really owns anything. (I can use this in my film to show how Angela's basic philosophy is directly opposed to the greed that inspires the power brokers to encroach on native rights.)

LOSS

Angela was devastated by her mother's death. She won't let go of her feelings of sadness. In the movie, she learns to deal with loss in healthy ways and her character arc actually shows how she learns to accept loss as part of life and move on to other things.

You can see how, by creating an emotional biography, I've given myself material that could give rise to screenplay scenes in which my character could develop and reveal herself. During the writing process, I could use the ways in which Angela became sensitive to native issues as a child to create ways in which the audience might become sensitive to those same issues. The biography could provide me with an actual process to draw audiences into the issue. I might even include flashbacks to Angela's past to make situations in her present more dramatic.

Notice how this emotional biography also influences how Angela reacts to other characters in the film. Using the emotional response certain characters might bring out in her, will add sub-text and a definite richness to the film.

Biography Exercises

1. Create a personal image map/biography and emotional biography of your main characters using the template above.

Feeling/Reaction Exercise

2. Once you become ultra familiar with your characters by preparing image maps/biographies, you'll need to further focus your social issue stance by developing your main characters' feelings about, and reaction to, specific external issues that might play a part in your screenplay. For example, if your characters are dealing with injustice, you'll need to know how they "handle" that and why.

For example, in my Native Rights screenplay, Angela might be profoundly disturbed by injustice since she first saw her mother having to deal with a nosy neighbor who accused her of neglecting Angela. Angela knew the accusation was unfair. She wasn't neglected but her mother left her alone a lot because she worked two jobs to provide for her.

Using the template below, just as you did with emotions, write paragraphs on your main character's feelings about, reaction to, the following:

- Gender
- Poverty
- Wealth
- Injustice
- Violence
- Honesty/Truth
- Pleasure
- Pain

If you've done these exercises, your knowledge of your main characters should be pretty complete. That knowledge will make your screenplay stronger. To prove that point, let's examine how character propelled and informed the story of some very successful social issue films.

5

ON THE SHOULDERS
OF GIANTS

I've chosen six social issues from the social issue list and linked them with five classic social issue films to show how a main character's interaction with an issue moves the story of that issue forward. If we take a closer look at these films, we find that they are memorable not just because of the statements they make about social issues but also because of how the films' characters reacted to their issue-driven situations or became emblematic of the issue in some way. The characters in these films were so well drawn that they garnered Academy Awards or Nominations for the actors who played them.

Labor Practices: *Norma Rae*

Norma Rae (starring Sally Field, written by Harriet Frank Jr. and Irving Ravetch, directed by Martin Ritt, 1979) has become an iconic pro-union film. It's so inspiring because it shows us how an uneducated Southern cotton mill worker who commits to a noble cause (the union) even against mammoth opposition (from bosses, townspeople, co-workers, friends and family) can make a huge difference in her world. Audiences find her basic character traits of courage, feisty-ness, and tenacity laudable and at the same time sympathize with her vulnerability and personal problems. Norma's character is based in part on Crystal Lee Sutton, a real person who was fired from her job in a North Carolina plant for trying to organize a union.[1]

Our hearts go out to Norma Rae in the film's first few scenes. We see her in a hell-hole of a factory—deafening noise, huge dangerous-looking complicated machines chugging along, the air rife with floating fibers and fluff. She looks small and vulnerable although her body language tells us she's very capable and knows what she's doing. During her break, she discovers her mother (also a mill worker) has gone deaf from the noise. She confronts the factory doctor who belittles the problem. We sense right away that Norma Rae is a character who won't take abuse and who confronts injustice when she can even though she may be powerless to change it.

As we get to know Norma Rae, we learn she isn't perfect. She's single and has two children. She lives with her parents. She's having an affair with a married man. She resents the protective attitude of her doting father. She's a loud mouth and more than a little brash.

When Reuben Warshowski, a Jewish big city Union Organizer (Ron Leibman) comes from New York to unionize the mill workers we know she'd be the perfect person to help him. Like Norma, Reuben is smart, courageous and committed to ending injustice in the workplace. Norma is suspicious but curious enough to watch him closely. Gradually, he earns her trust and even though they come from different worlds, we cheer when she decides to join him in his crusade to turn the cotton mill into a union shop.

Screenwriters Frank and Ravetch could have chosen to show audiences the process by which companies become unionized by making the union organizer the main character. They could have had us follow Reuben as he suffered defeats and intimidations and finally as he gained the trust of the workers. This would have been a nice enough story. We could have sympathized with this do-gooder and watched him take his lumps on the way to becoming a local hero.

Instead, they chose to make Norma Rae the main character and in so doing created a much grittier and relate-able movie. As we watch Norma Rae suffering in the horrible heat and noise of the factory, we sweat and suffer with her. We can understand her outrage and the outrage of her co-workers as they are denied small "rights"—bathroom breaks, access to drinking fountains, safety equipment and health precautions.

As witnesses to the character's poverty, we realize how dependent she and her whole community are on the cotton mill. We realize mill jobs are the only ones available in the dirt-poor town and without those jobs people would starve. That makes us understand why Norma and the mill workers endure harsh plant conditions and terrible treatment from the company bosses.

As the film progresses, we can understand why Reuben, the union organizer, and Norma need each other. Reuben, who's never worked in a factory and has had all the benefits of education, has difficulty getting support from plant workers who can't connect with him. Norma Rae's family has worked in the mill for generations, but she simply can't see a way out even though she's desperately tired of the workplace horrors. Norma Rae and Reuben support and make each other more effective.

Reuben molds Norma Rae. He comforts her after her married boyfriend slaps her around. He tells her she's smart. He encourages her. He teaches her to exercise what rights she does have. He teaches her to write letters. He turns her on to Dylan Thomas and tells her stories of New York life and of other union struggles. As Norma Rae admits, "he's in my head."

Norma Rae is a perfect acolyte. She's eager to learn, she respects Reuben's intelligence and education without being overwhelmed by it, she agrees that there should be a way to stop the workplace problems and she appreciates his commitment to the cause and his sincerity. She's happy to try to make things easier for him by being his advocate in the workplace and assuring people he's trustworthy. All along the way Reuben inspires Norma Rae. She sees Reuben standing up to the bosses and is impressed. She hears his philosophy and gets him to boil it down so everyone can understand it. She's thrilled that Reuben appreciates and likes her.

But that doesn't mean Reuben and Norma get it on. This is a really important aspect of the film. It's vital that the audience understand that Norma Rae is not taking on the union cause because she's in love with Reuben or because she's anticipating a relationship with him. Lots of screenwriters might have given us the knee-jerk cliché of the union organizer/mill worker love affair fueling this story.

Frank and Ravetch wisely side-stepped this pitfall by giving Norma Rae a loving husband (Beau Bridges) whose opposition to her long hours and over-blown dedication to the union provides extra tension in Norma Rae's struggle. The audience sees that in spite of mounting personal pressures at home, she's still committed to the union and that commitment becomes clearer and stronger as the film progresses even though her friendship with Reuben grows.

When Reuben and Norma Rae skinny dip in a pond, Norma Rae does teasingly flirt with Reuben but he stays friendly and neutral. We suspect she's only testing his sincerity to the cause. Reuben and Norma Rae never even hug. At the film's end when they've achieved their goal and Reuben is leaving, they only shake hands. Watching it, I yearned to have them hug but I understood that the hand shake re-inforced Rubin and Norma Rae's important "business" relationship. This hand shake closes the film on an altruistic level. Because of their friends-only relationship, Reuben reminds Norma Rae that she is valued for her smarts, not for her body and that she is more than just the sexual object she always believed herself to be. And that hand shake also makes sure that *Norma Rae* stays a film about how a cotton mill worker becomes empowered enough to unionize her place of work. Audiences are left with the nobility and triumph of that.

Norma Rae's the one who mobilizes the workers. Reuben is an outsider and no matter how hard he tries, he simply can't get their attention. It's because of Norma Rae's character that the union movement in the mill gathers steam. And finally, it's her tenacity and guts that gives the film its most iconic image—an image that still resonates with pro-union forces today.

Norma Rae is finally fired because she defies her bosses and copies a racially inflammatory notice they've posted. She refuses to leave until the sheriff comes to escort her home. In the meantime, in the middle of the incredibly noisy and busy factory, she gets up on a table, draws the word "union" on a piece of cardboard and stands holding the sign up over her head. It's a thrilling and declarative moment. Because of that culminating defiant act, and all the other small ones that have come before, her co-workers, one-by-one, slowly support her by turning off their machines until finally, against a background of steam and pipes, she's holding up the union sign in complete silence.

The "real" Norma Rae—Crystal Lee Sutton—did exactly that before she was dragged out of the J.P. Stevens Plant in Roanoke Rapids, North Carolina. The iconic image of that action immortalized in *Norma Rae* says it all: the battle for workers' rights can only be taken on by individuals with commitment and courage. And that's how Norma Rae's character made audiences champion this social issue.

Gay and Discrimination Issues: *Philadelphia*

Philadelphia (starring Tom Hanks and Denzel Washington, written by Ron Nyswaner, directed by Jonathan Demme, 1993) was inspired by the true story of Geoffrey Bowers, an attorney who in 1987 sued the law firm Baker and McKenzie for unfair dismissal in one of the first Aids discrimination cases. The film makers didn't bother to get the rights to Bowers' story. (We'll talk about this process in the next chapter.) When the film came out, Bowers' family recognized some of the scenes that seemed to exactly mimic scenes in Bowers' life. Even though Bowers had died, his family sued Tristar. After five days of testimony, Tristar settled with the family for an undisclosed amount.[2]

The fact that the lawsuit went as far as it did is a curious irony. How absurd that a movie about injustice ended up dealing out its own form of injustice. The film makers should have obtained the rights to Bowers' story or settled with the family immediately. That way they could have shown that those who make movies about social issues are themselves ethical and socially responsible. Unfortunately, that's not always the case.

Philadelphia was one of the first big-budget star-driven mainstream movies about AIDS and it was a hot potato. In the 1996 documentary *The Celluloid Closet,* Tom Hanks said that some of the more intimate scenes between Andrew Beckett (played by Hanks) and his lover Miguel (played by Antonio Banderis) were cut.

Even sanitized, the film was controversial and exposed the absurd prevailing attitude at the time—that all people with AIDS were homosexual and were to be shunned and AIDS was a contagious disease. It also exposed "underground" homophobia—the kind people won't talk about openly. These kinds of homophobes make jokes and snide remarks but seldom expose themselves as the haters they are.

When *Philadelphia* opens, two lawyers (Andrew Beckett and Joe Miller played by Denzel Washington) are arguing a case before a judge. Homosexuality is not an issue and that immediately leads the unsuspecting audience comfortably into the film. In fact, as we come to know Andrew Beckett we see him as nothing more than a great lawyer. We do see that he's in some sort of treatment but we're not really sure what that's for. Gradually though, with talk of T-cells and other chatter, we gather he has AIDS. By then, because of how we know the character in his professional life, that seems a background issue as does the fact that he's gay. And so it stays until we watch his illness getting worse and see him being fired.

Because Andrew is so sympathetic, smart and charming—all traits that Hanks himself brings to the table in his "star-like" persona—the audience is totally on his side and doesn't care what his illness or sexual preference might be. Eventually, Joe Miller, an admitted homophobe, doesn't either. When Andrew tells Joe he wants to sue his law firm for discriminatory dismissal, Joe is taken aback. He admits to falling prey to the current social misconception that AIDS is communicable through clothing or a handshake. So why does he take Andrew's case?

That's answered skilfully in the sub-text. In the original script, Joe Miller was NOT described as being African American. That doesn't mean that the screenwriter was averse to mentioning race in the script. The paralegal that works in Andrew's firm is described as being black but Miller is not. This leads us to the assumption that casting Denzel Washington in the role was a directorial decision and it was a wise one. By casting Denzel Washington as Joe Miller, director Jonathan Demme made the audience understand that as a black man, Joe could identify with Andrew as a victim of discrimination. Although Joe never talks about that, when he sees Andrew in the law library being asked to move to a private room, his expression indicates what he feels—that segregation of any kind and for any reason is wrong and illegal. He still fights with himself over his admitted homophobia, but in the end his sense of fairness and justice wins out.

We can almost sense the kind of image map/biography the Joe Miller character might have even though it's not spelled out for us. In that image map/biography, there could have been multiple scenes of discrimination that Joe might have faced on the way to becoming a successful lawyer. Washington as a black actor also most probably used events in his own life to convey the character's emotions at that time and it made the film relate-able and real.

On August 1, 2011 the *Los Angeles Times* printed a story on its *Late Extra* page about a black lawyer representing a former white supremacist. Milton Grimes, a 65-year-old black lawyer who represented Rodney King in federal court and two black O.J. Simpson jurors who had been dismissed, says he studied law because he wanted to represent black people during the civil rights movement. In spite of that, he is defending an ex-skinhead.

Grimes says Chad Brian Scott's tattoos and white supremacist affiliations have stereotyped him. "I will fight for him as I will fight for a black man," says Grimes who says that his client "reminds me of so many young minority men whose freedoms are arbitrarily taken away because of the color of their skin."[3] It's easy to see a movie here! And it relates to Joe Miller's motivation for taking Andrew Beckett's case in *Philadelphia.*

And by the way, earlier I said that you shouldn't write a movie whose main character is so hooked into a star that no one else can play that role. Arguably, *Philadelphia* might be an exception because Tom Hanks (who by then had played in *Sleepless in Seattle, League of their Own, Turner and Hooch* and *Big* among others) and Denzel Washington (who'd by then been in *Pelican Brief, Malcolm X* and *Mississippi Massala*) in the major roles, both superstars, gave this controversial movie its credibility.

People who probably wouldn't have gone to see this film with unknowns, were drawn into the theater perhaps on the strength of these two names and that helped to make *Philadelphia* (made for $25 million) a financial success with $77,446,440 total box office. In addition, their powerful performances ensured that the movie was a critical success. Hanks, particularly spectacular, won the Oscar (his first) that year for best actor. The characters in the film drove the issue and made the public understand that discrimination against AIDS patients is wrong and that homophobia that leads to discrimination in practice is illegal and hateful.

Censorship: *Good Morning Vietnam*

Good Morning Vietnam (starring Robin Williams and Forest Whitaker, written by Mitch Markowitz, directed by Barry Levinson, 1983) is another one of those character-driven social issue films that is hugely dependent on its star. Robin Williams was made for the role of Adrian Cronauer—a real military DJ who served during the Vietnam War. Cronauer was a maverick—a fast-talking, hard-driving wacky funny man who also happened to be a member of Mensa. Robin Williams, no slouch in the brain department either, had been making a name for himself (*Mork and Mindy, SCTV Moscow on the Hudson*) as a fast-talking, hard-driving comic with wild and wacky ways. He was famous for his ad-lib patter and the jokes that just flew off the top of his head.

Williams, who ad-libbed his radio broadcasts in the movie, effectively becomes Cronauer and is entirely believable and likeable as he does that. His free-wheeling style also emphasizes how out of control Cronauer can be.

The first time we see Cronauer, he's coming down the steps of a plane and he's wearing a big over-sized shirt, baggy pants, a white cardigan and funny cap that makes him look like a Greek peasant. We clearly get the idea that he isn't the typical military type. As Cronauer takes the air, it becomes obvious that he's not your average DJ either. He's a flamboyant, take-no-prisoners wise guy—a 1960s equivalent of a shock jock. He plays rock'n'roll instead of easy listening. He makes fun of Nixon, Johnson and the Army. He even (shudder, gasp) makes fun of the Vietnamese weather! He tells it like it is. And that of course doesn't sit well with the establishment uptight career military guys running the station who want everything to be controlled, calm and banal. The more flamboyant Cronauer becomes, the more the censors get down on him.

As the audience increasingly identifies with and likes Cronauer, it becomes more and more frustrated with the censorship he is forced to endure. This frustration is mirrored by auxiliary characters like his aide Ed Garlick (Forest Whitaker) the perfect Cronauer foil who tries to keep him out of trouble but can't help going along with his antics, and fellow DJ Marty Lee Dreiwitz (Robert Wuhl) who loves what Cronauer does, but is afraid to imitate him.

The censorship against Cronauer seems entirely unreasonable, partly because it's fueled by the jealousy of the wannabe comic Lt. Steven Hauk (Bruno Kirby). Kirby is hilarious and believable as the stiff-backed not-funny sergeant addicted to polkas and since he is such an unlikeable character, the odious nature of the censorship he imposes is further reinforced.

Particularly galling is the way in which the military censors prevent the troops in the field from knowing current information. In those days, without the internet and cell-phones, it was possible to keep the troops ignorant. Cronauer's social conscience finds this unfair and unjust and so when he reports unauthorized material, the audience cheers even though it means he's punished for it.

It's to Robin Williams' credit as an actor (he got his first Oscar nomination for this performance) that he's able to demonstrate Cronauer's soft side. When he performs "live" from a jeep to troops going off to the battle zone, the audience recognizes Cronauer's concern and love for them and the pity he feels for each one of them. He covers his heartbreak with humor and comes out looking like a hero. Williams' acting skills (where he's able to be serious) were later demonstrated in 1989 in *Dead Poets Society* (he was nominated for an Oscar), in 1991 in *The Fisher King* (he was again nominated for an Oscar) and in 1997 in *Good Will Hunting* (he won the Oscar for Best Actor).

Watching *Good Morning Vietnam*, audiences get the message that the Vietnam war was unjust, that censorship (often personally or politically motivated) is wrong, and that sometimes, in bad situations, humor does much to soothe, comfort and uplift. Cronauer as Williams plays him becomes a different sort of war hero, but a war hero nonetheless—one who stands up for truth and justice and who does what he can to help make a bad situation better regardless of personal cost.

Euthanasia: *Million Dollar Baby*

The main characters in the last three movies were based on or inspired by real people. The main characters in *Million Dollar Baby* (starring Clint Eastwood and Hillary Swank, written by Paul Haggis, directed by Clint Eastwood, 2004) were fictional. The movie was adapted from a short story by FX Toole (a fight manager and cut man whose real name is Jerry Boyd).

It's a sports story about Frankie Dunn, a boxing trainer (Clint Eastwood) and Maggie Fitzgerald, a female boxer (Hillary Swank) who talks him into training her. Maggie is a woman with nothing to lose. She's from a dirt poor dysfunctional family and boxing is the thing that gives purpose and meaning to her life. She works as a waitress, swiping the food people have left on their plates just so she can eat and at the same time save her pennies to join Frankie's gym and to buy equipment.

Frankie doesn't hold with women boxing. He thinks it's a freak show and his mantra is "I don't train girls!" He comes off as a hard and tough guy. But there's another side to him. He's learning Gaelic and he likes to take care of people—especially his fighters. That's emphasized through his relationship with Eddie, a broken-down boxer (Morgan Freeman won the Oscar for this role), who helps run his gym and his tolerance of Danger (Jay Baruchel), a wacky dumb fighter who spends time in his gym because he has no place else to go. Frankie is also a practicing Catholic—he prays and goes to Mass every day, but questions the Church's tenets so much it drives his priest to use four-letter words. This is important character information that makes the end of the film work.

Ostensibly, the film is about the relationship between Maggie and Frankie and their inner struggles. Euthanasia doesn't come up until the third act and that's what makes this social issue movie unique and interesting. The issue is introduced so late it gives the film its big punch ending and we're left on the mat gasping for air.

Based on the close relationship we've seen develop throughout the film, we come to understand the characters and their motivations and we come to see why they both buy into the ultimate end. For Maggie, paralyzed during a fight, her leg amputated, life without boxing isn't feasible. She makes that clear in an expository speech she makes to Frankie when she tries for the umpteenth time to convince him how important boxing is to her. The speech is effectively her image map/biography and is super expository. This kind of exposition is something writers are always warned against, but in this case and in this place in the movie it's entirely appropriate. I use it in my classes as an example of simple and dead-on exposition that is justified.

MAGGIE

I'm 32 Mr. Dunn and I'm here celbratin' the fact that
I spent another year scrapin' dishes and waitressin'
which I've been doin' since 13 and according to you,
I'll be 37 before I can ever throw a decent punch
which after workin' this feed bag for a month I know
I should realize God's simple truth. The other truth is
that my brother's in prison, my sister cheats on
welfare by pretendin' one of her babies is still alive,
my daddy's dead and my momma weighs 312 pounds.
If I was thinkin' straight, I'd go back home buy a deep
fryer and some oreos. The problem is this is the only
thing I ever felt good doin'. If I'm too old for this,
then I got nothin'. That enough truth to suit you?

Because of that speech, his gradually softening heart and his penchant
for protecting strays, Frankie agrees to train her but says he's not going
to care what happens to her.

FRANKIE

... don't come crying to me if you get hurt.
    ... I'll teach you all you need to know and you go
off and make a million dollars. I don't care. You get
your teeth knocked out. I don't care. I don't want to
hear about it either way.

Gradually though, as her training goes on and she improves (12
straight knockouts), we see that he does come to care, and very much.
He admires her courage, her talent, her determination and her refusal
to quit. He understands it. When she breaks her nose during a fight,
and he wants to let the ring doctor stop it, she convinces him she can
win if he'll re-set her nose and stop the bleeding. He does this against
his better judgment. (A fore-shadowing of the ending.) She goes on to
win the fight and that's when he gives her a Gaelic pet name (Mo
Cuishle). When they travel to Europe for the big fight, he puts it on
her robe and her team's jackets and hires pipers to pipe her into the
ring but refuses to tell her what the name means.

When Frankie takes Maggie home to watch her present a house to her ungrateful, horrible white trash mother, he realizes he's become her only real family and that she's stepped into the role of his daughter from whom he is estranged. This is reinforced in the third act when her no-good family visits Maggie in the hospital and tries to get her to sign away her assets. In as mean a scene as has ever been written, her mother shoves a pen into Maggie's mouth (she's a quadriplegic on a breathing tube) and tells her to sign away everything to the family. The fact that Maggie refuses and throws her mother out is confirmation that essentially, Frankie is the only "family" she has left.

We can see that he takes his responsibility seriously. He's at the hospital day and night and experiences unbearable pain when he learns of her leg amputation and attempted suicides.

We know that helping Maggie die is a tough decision for Frankie and one he doesn't want to make. And yet he does it because he puts himself in her shoes and understands what boxing means to her. When his priest tells him that helping her die will eternally damn his soul, Frankie doesn't back down. He's willing to sacrifice himself for her as a parent would for a child. In her final moments, as a declaration of his love for her, he finally tells Maggie that Mo Cuishle means my blood, my darling. A fifteen Kleenex moment!

The validity of Frankie's action is something the audience will have to struggle with just as Frankie struggles as he leaves town to begin a nomadic life—the life of someone who feels like a fugitive. Or does he? This social issue movie really brings up many possibilities for discussion and soul searching about euthanasia and, again, the fact that it's introduced at the film's end makes it overwhelmingly compelling. By the time we get to it, we're so involved with the characters and so engaged by their wants and needs that we go through Frankie's inner turmoil with him—and that's exactly what we're supposed to do. We see the situation from Maggie's perspective and understand why she tries to bleed to death by biting her tongue. Maggie's character is so convincing (Swank won the Oscar) that we're on her side. But we also see the situation from Frankie's perspective (Eastwood was nominated for an Oscar for his performance) as he struggles with his feelings and considers a young life wasted, potential denied and a person he loves suffering unbearably. We understand why both people want a clean end to their pain.

This is clearly a film about people confronting a bad situation and making a serious social-issue decision; whether or not we agree with what they choose to do, our relationship with them makes us think deeply and seriously about their issue—in this case euthanasia. You couldn't ask for more in a social issue film.

Abortion: *Vera Drake*

Vera Drake (starring Imelda Staunton and Jim Broadbent. Written and directed by Mike Leigh, 2004) is quite remarkable because it explores the issue of abortion form the point of view of the abortionist. And this is an unusual abortionist indeed. Vera Drake (magnificently played by Imelda Staunton who was nominated for an Oscar) is a dowdy and mild-mannered middle-aged housewife who goes about doing good deeds in 1950s England. She's sweet and efficient—a woman who cleans houses and gives an extra bit of love and care to those who need it. She brings soup to a lonely sick neighbor and does his shopping. She pampers her family and friends. And on the side she helps girls "in trouble."

Vera doesn't think this is a big deal. She doesn't even really see herself as an abortionist. She just believes she's just helping bring on women's periods. She doesn't let herself think that her methods (grating carbolic soap into a tub of water and injecting it into the vagina of a pregnant woman) are actually aborting a fetus. And she doesn't tell her family what she's doing because probably, in her heart of hearts, she knows it's wrong. Certainly she's aware that it's illegal which is why she doesn't talk about it. And she certainly doesn't solicit clients or take money. A friend of hers does that. No. What Vera does, she does out of the goodness of her heart.

When one of her "patients" nearly dies, her involvement comes out and she's arrested. When this happens, she's shocked and ashamed. She can't stop crying. Her family is appalled. Her sister-in-law refuses to speak to her again. She becomes a social pariah. We're as shocked as she is at her arrest because we've seen that she's a good and simple woman with no real malice or intent. Even the police feel sorry that she must be punished, emphasizing the antiquated nature of the abortion laws and the problems and misery they caused (and would still cause were these laws were to be reintroduced).

Vera's motives are clearly personal. Without saying so, she gives us a glimpse into her image map/biography by sobbing when her police interrogator asks if she once had an abortion herself. By her body language, we suspect that someone might have indeed given her an abortion using the same methods she uses. Perhaps she was so grateful that she was compelled to help other women in the same way. Or perhaps she was in need of an abortion and never had it and her life was ruined because of it. She does have two children. Perhaps one of them is the product of that unwanted pregnancy. We can only speculate because Vera doesn't say anything. She only cries but that crying intimates a great deal.

In the third act, when Vera's in prison, she meets other abortionists. They are hardened women who are multiple offenders. She seems bewildered by them and doesn't see herself as part of their group. As she climbs the stairs to her cell, hugging her sweater around her, we suspect that Vera has "learned her lesson" but still isn't convinced that she deserves her punishment.

Clearly, *Vera Drake* is a period piece depicting the way things were in the 1950s but it definitely serves as a cautionary tale for the present in the face of movements intending to repeal laws that would allow women to obtain safe clinical abortions on demand. While audiences who are anti-abortion may believe in overturning current laws that allow abortion, and might abhor the acts committed by Vera Drake, those who come to know and feel for her can't help sympathizing with her in this film. That's because Mike Leigh has provided us all with a brilliant look at another side of the abortion issue. This film, sympathetic to the well-meaning abortionist, at the same time derides the law that made Vera Drake do the things she did.

6

TRUE OR FALSE?

Legal Precautions

Usually, social issue stories have more punch if they are true and that means that a writer can always find his/her way into a social issue by using the true stories of real people. But keep in mind that how close the writer keeps to the actual story is a point of contention in today's film community. Because your film is NOT a documentary, you might find it necessary to "fudge" some of the facts for dramatic effect or to change the story so that the process and outcome speak to the point you are trying to make. As T.S. Eliot said in *Burnt Norton*, "human kind cannot bear very much reality."[1] Everything you see is not what it seems. Some stories, entirely true, aren't interesting enough to audiences. Some are even too amazing to be believed. And most, in their progress, don't have enough dramatic effect to be movies. Some of the facts and situations may be dramatic, but to make them come alive, writers are forced to add, invent and augment and embellish stories.

Some people take exception to this kind of "fudging." This is particularly true when it comes to dramatizations of "real" events. For example, when Oliver Stone made *JFK* (his 1991 film about the Kennedy Assassination), he said in an article by Roger Ebert in the *Chicago Sun Times*, that he found it to be "a distressing experience. It was disturbing to have this film attacked so early" and went on to say that "a lot of people are attacking my credibility."

In this article, Ebert recounted that "Dan Rather had attacked the film on CBS, the *Washington Post* had printed and criticized some of the screenplay, political pundit Tom Wicker had written a negative cover story in the *New York Times* arts section and *Newsweek* had splashed across its cover, 'Why Oliver Stone's new movie can't be trusted.' They felt Stone's movie was based on unsupportable speculation and they believed his film's hero, former New Orleans' District Attorney Jim Garrison, was an unscrupulous publicity seeker who drummed up his celebrated case against Clay Shaw out of thin air."[2]

In that same article, Stone defended himself by saying that his was an "artistic interpretation of events." Nevertheless, Stone admitted that he embellished and changed facts to coincide with his theory of the assassination.

Unfortunately, even though *JFK* was not a documentary, people who saw it believed it to be entirely true. And that's the problem with lots of docudramas. Audiences tend to believe that what they see on the screen really happened, especially if a prominent news story is involved. Even though the film makers might add a disclaimer, it's still a battle for the audience to tell the difference between truth and fiction.

For example, audiences may have believed the recent Oscar winning film *The Social Network* was an actual picture of Jeff Zukerberg, the founder of Facebook, particularly since it was "inspired" by *The Accidental Billionaires: The Founding of Facebook, A Tale of Sex, Money Genius, and Betrayal*, a 2009 book by Ben Mezrich about the founding of Facebook.

It wasn't. Even though the book and the script were written at the same time, writer Adam Sorkin took substantial liberties to make his character more movie-worthy. *New York Magazine* writer Mark Harris asked Sorkin if it was fair that "many of us may walk away from the movie not simply thinking that he has created an extraordinary character but that we are, in fact, seeing the real Mark Zuckerberg." Sorkin replied:

> When you're writing nonfiction that's always a question that you're wrestling with, especially when you're writing about people who are still alive. On one hand, you don't want to screw around with people's lives, you never want to say anything that isn't true, and you don't want to mess with history. On the other hand, this isn't a documentary. Art isn't about what happened, and the properties of people and the properties of

characters are two completely different things. There's a set of facts I'm dealing with, and I try to imagine motivations and fill in blanks that none of us can see. But the question of truth—the very first words out of Mark's mouth in the present-day part of the movie are: 'That's not what happened.' And that's my signal to the audience that there are going to be any number of unreliable narrators. This isn't the movie that's going to tell you Mark Zuckerberg stole Facebook or that he didn't. But . . . we would sure love for those arguments to happen in the parking lot.[3]

Making things up about a real person (or an event) for the good of the movie may be artistically sound but is it ethical? Many would say no. Certainly, the actual people involved in movies based on true stories might not be happy. Some might (and have) even sued. But film makers get away with it by using the "inspired by true events" label. If your story is only "inspired by" it doesn't have to be "true." That means that you can make your point as outrageously as you want to just as long as you make it. (There are some exceptions we'll discuss later.) But that's a rather ruthless way of looking at things and it certainly worked with *Social Network*. Aaron Sorkin won the Oscar for best adapted screenplay in 2010, even though it was fiction inspired by a book that was purportedly factual.

Awards aside, you should know that in a social issue movie, if your story is true and you distort facts or blatantly lie, you'll lose lots of credibility and could do actual harm to your cause. In thinking that the end justifies the means and that you'll get lots of publicity for that cause, you could wind up turning off the very people you want to rally.

This entire issue is highlighted by the court kerfuffle involving the Oscar Winning Best Picture of 2010 *The Hurt Locker* about the rigors and horrors of war. The producers of the film along with the director Katherine Bigelow and screenwriter Mark Boal are being sued by Iraq war veteran Master Sgt. Jeffrey Sarver for misappropriation of his publicity rights, defamation, breach of contract and infliction of emotional distress. The *Hollywood Reporter* said that on August 8, 2011, a District Judge "expressed an inclination to dismiss all claims except the one where Sarver alleges that his likeness was misappropriated by the film makers."

If the judge's tentative opinion stands, it means that Sarver won't have an opportunity to test before a jury his theory that even a character in a purportedly fictional film can be libelous nor his allegation that when (screenwriter) Boal was embedded with the U.S. military to research an article for *Playboy Magazine*, he agreed to 'ground rules,' including restrictions on the type of personal information that Boal could report on a service member. On the other hand, if a judge allows the case to go forward on the publicity rights claim, Sarver will have overcome one obstacle in his lawsuit against the film's producers who had argued Sarver's claims were precluded by the First Amendment . . . The attorney for Bigelow and Boal argued that allowing the case to go forward would have a chilling effect on film making and that it would directly impact artists, directors, film makers in the future.[4]

It's all quite a mess and it seems like screenwriters are over a barrel. On one hand they want to create a meaningful and great story that will draw in audiences and get them involved in a real situation so they can take real action. On the other hand, as people of conscience, screenwriters who are writing social issue films really don't want to lie, distort or misrepresent a cause for the sake of creating big box-office receipts.

That's why it might behoove screenwriters to get the rights to people's stories. If you are basing your movie on a book, you also need to get the rights. In order to do that, you should employ an entertainment attorney who knows the ropes. When I asked attorney Jay Dougherty about the necessity of acquiring rights to people's lives and stories, he agreed that even though "no one owns his life story," it is advisable to acquire certain waivers and rights.

Mr. Dougherty, a Loyola Law school (Los Angeles) professor, is an expert in copyright law and the right of publicity. He's worked as a senior executive at Twentieth Century Fox Film Corporation, MGM, UA, Morgan Creek Productions and Turner Broadcasting Systems. He's handled legal work on many fact-based or fact-inspired films and negotiated numerous life-story rights agreements.

He says:

> You're allowed to tell true stories as long as you don't disclose highly embarrassing facts about the people you're talking about. You don't need

a waiver to tell an inoffensive story. Not all states even recognize the right of privacy. But because the legal issues can be complex, and it's difficult to change a person's identity if your film deals with a distinctive event, it's always simpler from a legal point of view if the person you're writing about gives you a release or waiver. Sometimes you 'buy' life story rights, but you aren't buying property rights. Instead, you're getting explicit permission to fictionalize the person, to mix fact and fiction, use their name and they are essentially giving you permission to defame them and invade their privacy.

Professor Dougherty explains that because the person may not want you to fictionalize his story, hurt his feelings or portray him in a less than favorable light, it's necessary to negotiate with him and that's where money comes into play. You'll need to make a deal that looks like an option/purchase of rights agreement offering a small amount of money to develop your project and then ultimately buy the rights later for an additional amount of money. You may also offer a payment for consulting services and for an assurance that he will disclose additional information and also agree not to talk to other people.

There are typically two types of paper work—a short release document that is a waiver of claims and a release from liability , or a longer "life story rights agreement," containing the release and other provisions. These waivers and releases are required by producers to get insurance on the picture and to avoid legal difficulties later on. Professor Dougherty says, "Errors and commission insurance—also called 'E&C' or producer's liability insurance—requires the producer to follow certain legal clearance procedures and one of those requires getting releases for any individual identified in your film unless you can convince the insurance company you don't need them. If you're dealing with a dead person most of this goes away. The heirs don't have a claim against what anyone says about their dead relatives, at least under U.S. law." (The one type of claim that under some states' laws, doesn't end on death is right of publicity. In that claim, heirs can argue that a relative is being used for commercial benefit, but generally use in a film would not be that kind of commercial benefit.)

"Waivers need to be really specific and clear," says Professor Dougherty. He cautioned that it is important to make these waivers simple and understandable so that the person signing them knows what's involved. "There have been cases," he said, "where people sued because they claimed they didn't know what they were signing and they won their case. The onus is on the person coming up with the waiver to make it clear. However, wavers and releases are usually written to favor the producer who may be paying to be able to fictionalize the story to make it more dramatic and interesting. It can even allow the film makers to make up false things about the person in question but that should be stated clearly."

Some people will try to get around acquiring rights by using the "inspired by" label. The question there becomes whether anybody could make the claim that they are recognized in the film and that false facts or embarrassing private facts were revealed. Sometimes, Professor Dougherty goes on to say, even if something is private and highly embarrassing, if it is a matter of legitimate public interest there is no violation of privacy rights. In the U.S., the matter of legitimate public interest is broad especially as to government officials and celebrities. In some foreign countries, there is a bigger zone of intimacy and if your film involves a person from abroad, there is a greater risk that you may be liable in the country where that person has residency. In Britain, for example, libel laws are more favorable to the plaintiff in such cases; in Germany, privacy rights may be stronger against a media portrayal than in the U.S. However, if the defendant's assets are in the U.S., a U.S. Court may not enforce collection on a foreign court judgment. In the U.S. entertainment is considered speech and laws aren't allowed to restrict most speech.

The bottom line is that it's important to consult a lawyer and far less problematic to acquire rights and waivers. Putting up some money now will save you much grief later. It will also ensure that you are in some way attached to the project. If you don't get things legally straight and put something in writing, there's always a good possibility that you'll be thrown off the project or circumvented in another way. Of course, that may happen anyway. Lots of people who've acquired timed options on stories have been dismayed to discover that large production companies were waiting in the wings for those options to run out so they could swoop down and grab the rights for themselves. By offering large amounts of money, these raiders can effectively hijack stories away from screenwriters who've spent months cultivating their subjects and working on screenplays. It's a fact of life and there's not much you can do about that except play on the trust and loyalty of your subject. If you're honest and fair and have developed a close relationship with your subject, that person might stick with you rather than sell out to ruthless big showbiz marauders who don't have the subject's best interests at heart. It could happen but if it doesn't, move on. Don't hold it against a person who has thousands of dollars dangled in front of him. Sometimes, the temptation is too much to bear and you can't really blame anyone for giving in.

Once you do get the rights, you need to decide how comfortable you are changing a person's story to make it saleable. What can you live with? You've got to decide for yourself what the stakes are. How much are you willing to embellish so the greater good of making a strong point is served? Or is the point strong enough in reality without the embellishment? It depends on your point and how subtle your story is. Chances are, if you found your way into a social issue by finding a true story, the truth will be compelling enough and you won't need to fictionalize.

But if you must embellish or make things up, do it with your characters and their reactions. If the people you based your story on are not as courageous as you'd like, you can make them more courageous. If they have no sense of humor, give them a quick wit. The real folks certainly won't mind the positive bumps and if there are enough of them, they might forgive the negative ones. You can push the character envelope where you might not want to push the fact envelope.

Lots of Participant's movies are based on real events. Jonathan King says that everyone struggles with the problem of what facts to change. "We're developing a movie about the Deep Water Horizon disaster when the rig exploded and sank. Everybody knows what happened after that. Oil poured into the gulf for months and months and months but not a lot of people know what happened that day so we optioned the rights to a New York Times article and the writer is writing a script based on that article. You can't know what happened in the minutes before and after it started to explode because all of the people who were there unfortunately are dead so you need to create all of this and you can take a certain amount of dramatic license about what people were saying to each other and who was standing where. We've all read the government report and the books, a ton of research but one thing that's been important to me in developing the movie is that there were a certain amount of real people on the rig and a certain number of real people who came off the rig and there's a certain amount of real people who did not make it off. We can't violate that. We aren't having people walk around in real life and then kill them in the movie. That's just wrong. We're using real names and we have to respect that absolutely. And then we're taking dramatic license with what happened. It's public information. Especially when you're dealing with a tragedy like that you'll figure something out about how to compensate the survivors and the victims but working it all out in advance is so complicated and potentially time consuming. It's legally unnecessary but you make the movie with the best intention of doing the right thing by the survivors.

You can source the information from multiple sources. We really didn't need to legally option the New York Times article but it came in a package and the way the writers of the article organized their thinking it's in some way copyright-able so we optioned the story.

When I asked screenwriter Susannah Grant (*Erin Brockovich, 28 Days, The Soloist*) about that struggle she said "with real stories I've found that it's less about changing things and more about choosing what you include. You can't include everything so once you figure out why you're telling the story, then you figure out which aspects of the life support that story. There's a difference between the facts and the truth. Like in *Erin Brockovich*. Erin missed a million birthday parties, she missed picking up her kids, she missed a lot and it was hard on the kids and hard on her. Showing a bunch of missed birthday parties is a bit boring but I needed to put that in so I put in a scene that never happened. She's driving home and George tells her that Beth said her first words and she missed it. It runs about a minute and it's so much more dramatic than relating the facts. So it's not factually correct but it's absolutely truthfully correct. There's always a way of narrowing it down to its essence because you only have two hours. Every scene has to be a Sherpa carrying its own pack and someone else's pack to really be earning its keep.

If you sincerely care about the real person you're writing about, you are going to do it to the best of your talent and ability you're going to do a truthful job and to spend the whole time worrying how they are going to feel . . . you can always change it and pull it back but if (during the writing) you're always saying I can't do that . . . you're going to be in big trouble.

The "trick" in writing a story based on true events is to listen to your conscience and to your heart. If you're in touch with both of these, then you'll know when you've crossed a line and you'll stop yourself before you go too far. We owe it to ourselves as writers and as people, to be able to live with ourselves and be proud of our work.

7

PLAN OF ATTACK

Now that you've chosen your issue and come up with characters (and perhaps story rights), you'll need to decide how you want to "attack" your subject without it coming across as preachy, maudlin or (God forbid!) boring. Of course, you'll want to present it in a way in which the audience can best relate to it. Some subjects do better with one approach than another. For example, imagine if *Hotel Rwanda* had been written as a comedy. An absurd idea but had it happened the serious issue of genocide would have been greatly diminished. Or if *Avatar* had been written as a trial movie! The issue of native people's land loss might have been emphasized, but all the magic of the movie would have been removed.

You need to carefully consider the depth and breadth of your social issue and decide what "model" you'll want to use to relate it. I'm using the word "model" rather than "genre" because even though you might write your movie in a genre: thriller, action/adventure, comedy etc., you'll use a social action movie model to deliver the issue.

To start, here's a list of the models with a brief description of each. We'll study them in more detail using examples, later.

The Sherlock/Snitch: The Investigation/ Whistleblower Model

This model unfurls the social issue through a process of investigation. The investigator can be the whistleblower or someone else who gets the whistleblower to talk. It can be written as an action-adventure, suspense or mystery.

The Lawyer-Up: The Trial Model

The social issue comes to light here in the process of accumulating trial evidence, winning a trial or conducting a trial. The trial doesn't have to take up most of the film, but the lawyer involved needs to be pursuing evidence using whistleblowers as witnesses and even investigators to make his/her case. Often, the trial doesn't take place until the third act but it's still a trial model because it centers on a lawyer and the legal process.

The Heart-Tugger: The Relationship Model

The social issue in this model acts as the catalyst for the relationship or drives it. The relationship can also be defined by the social issue. In this model, characters work out, around or through the issue as they work out their relationships.

The Chuckle: The Satirical Model

This movie needs to be funny, irreverent, ironic, outrageous and anything else you can think of to send up what's going on with the particular social issue. The issue itself can be serious (the hilarious *Dr. Strangelove* (1964) sends up (nuclear) war issues!) but it needs to be presented in a way that makes audiences take notice through laughter or a bemused head-shake. The humor can be dark and not necessarily guffaw-provoking.

The Life: The Biopic Model

The social issue in this model is part (or all) of a person's life story and drastically influences it either positively or negatively. The social issue doesn't have to take up all of the person's life but should be present in it enough so that it influences the person to become who they are at the end of the film.

The Yoda: The Mentor Model

This model emphasizes the social issue by using a mentor who guides his/her charge through the machinations of the social issue. The

Yoda does NOT make huge sacrifices in this struggle (the Shining Knight does that) but is rather in an elevated instructional or helping mode. That doesn't mean that the Yoda is unaffected by the issue. Just that his/her understanding is greater that the person who struggles with it.

The Shining Knight: The Hero/Rescuer Model

The social issue in this model is taken on by a hero and rescuer. This could be someone who has no particular stake in the issue but champions it (or the person involved in it) and also becomes involved because of compassion and the desire to make things right. The Shining Knight can also be someone deeply involved in the issue who, against all odds, takes on all challengers in an attempt to make things better for others.

Note: Be careful not to get the Yoda and Shining Knight confused. Remember that the Yoda is usually above the fray most of the time although occasionally dipping down into it for the sake of his acolyte while the Shining Knight is a warrior in the middle of the fray at all times and often acts as rescuer.

Keep in mind that you can blend models and combine models. For example you can write a script that combines *The Chuckle* with *The Lawyer-Up*, *The Sherlock/Snitch* with *The Knight in Shining Armor*, *The Heart-Tugger* with *The Yoda* and so on. Just remember that at all times you need to make sure that the way in which you combine models always showcases your social issue even though it may seem to be in the background of your story. That means the social issue you're writing about (what your movie is "really about") will be the "A" story of your film (the main plot). You can interject a "B" story (the sub-plot) in a different vein (thereby perhaps combining models somewhat) but your main approach will give the most weight to the social issue.

For example, *Philadelphia* demonstrates *The Heart-Tugger* even though it may at first seem like an example of *The Lawyer-Up*. That's because although the film is ostensibly "about" an anti-discrimination law suit (a gay social issue re discrimination) it's "*really about*" the relationship between Joe Miller and Andrew Beckett. As Joe breaks down his own homophobia, he's able to do that to participants in the courtroom and even though the movie starts with a trial and uses courtroom scenes, it's still an example of *The Heart-Tugger* Model with lots of *The Lawyer-Up* Model folded in. Since the movie is "really about" overcoming homophobia (gay issues), it turns out as the A story in the film even though the legal B story (discrimination issues) is a close second.

Combining models may sound complicated but it isn't if, as I said before, you're sure of what your movie is "really about." If you know that, you won't have a problem. *Philadelphia* is clearly about overcoming prejudice about AIDS and the gay people afflicted by it. It may feature a trial in which that prejudice is recognized and "punished" but because of the relationship between the two main characters, the ultimate message of the film hits home.

How can you "try out" your model? You can do it by creating what I call *Outline Magic*—a simple point form outline system I developed that works with structure to tell your story quickly and efficiently. In the past twenty-five years of teaching and writing, I've supervised nearly 2,000 scripts and each one of them falls into this natural pattern of storytelling. It's not exclusive to social issue screenplays. It can be used to write any kind of movie.

My *Outline Magic* system is a twenty-four-point outline that's brief, fluid and changeable. You can play with it as you write. It hits all the important structural points (as defined by Syd Field in his seminal 1979 book *Screenplay*) and provides a perfect vehicle for working quickly. It also works very well when you're working with development people because it's a very clear way of defining and planning the story. It's simple and easy. Here's how it works:

The story is outlined using plot points. A plot point is something that moves the action forward about every *five* movie minutes. It can be one scene or even two or three short scenes. Using the fact that one minute of screen time roughly equals one page of script, *one plot point will take about five pages.*

In the writing of the movie, you may find that some points take fewer pages and some more, but as a rule, the general page count is five pages a plot point. That means, in a two-hour movie, you've got *twenty-four* plot points to tell your story.

Here's the outline template that organizes the plot points in a two-hour movie into a format that's structure perfect.

Outline Magic Template
Full Length Screenplay 24-Point Outline

Act One *(Goal: To establish genre, characters, atmosphere, problem)*
1.
2. *(Page 10 hook)*
3. *(Page 15 inciting incident)*
4.
5.
6. **End of Act One (p. 30)**

Act Two *(Goal: To further develop characters, working on solving the problem with twists)*
7.
8.
9. **Second Act Spike #1 (p. 45)** *(substantial movement in early Act Two to propel attention)*
10.
11.
12. **Midpoint (p. 60)** *(The middle of the movie. Major move forward.)*
13.
14.
15. **Second Act Spike #2 (p. 75)** *(substantial movement to propel to end of act)*
16.
17.
18. **End of Act Two (p. 90)** *(Move toward Resolution and tie-up)*

Act Three *(Goal: To solve the problem, tie up relationships, bring home issues)*
19. Beginning of Act Three.
20.

21.

22.

23.

24.

When you're filling in the outline, you may not know all the plot points but you should definitely figure out the major points—(i.e. *plot point 6 (End of Act One p. 30), plot point 9 (Spike #1 in Act Two p. 45), plot point 12 (Midpoint p. 60), plot point 15 (Spike #2 in Act Two p. 75) and plot point 18 (the end of the Second Act p. 90)*.

For example, you may know plot points 1, 2, 3 but NOT 4 and 5 and then you may know 6 but NOT 7 and 8. The plot points you leave blank are where you can slot in your sub-plot. I'll demonstrate this later.

Use short sentences to create your outline. You may, if you like, include scenes in point form under the defining sentence. For example:

- John and Alfreda meet when John walks his pet dragon into Starbucks.
- They become entangled in the dragon leash.
- The dragon escapes as Alfreda faints (she's terrified of reptiles).
- John kisses her passionately. It's love at first sight and to hell with the dragon!

Remember that this outline is fluid. That means if you discover something vital or change your mind as you go along, you can simply change the plot points to reflect where you want the plot to go. Keep in mind too, that as you're writing and come up with new plot twists that have radical implications for what you've already written, make notes and keep writing as if you've already re-written the first act. If you do that, you'll be spared the horrible syndrome of constant first act re-writing. That syndrome—going back again and again until the first act is perfect—has kept many a writer working for years on a project that could have been finished and out the door.

Note: If you're writing a 90-minute movie, your template will vary slightly still keeping to structure: Act One will end at about pages 20–23, the first spike in Act Two will be on page 35, midpoint will be at page 45, the second spike will be at page 60 and the end of the second act will be at page 75. Act Three goes from pages 75–90. If your movie extends past two hours (not a good idea these days—studios hate that!) you'll shift your plot points accordingly to make the second act longer—sometimes by adding a third spike, and make the third act longer too.

Here's how I've outlined the first Act of one of my favorite movies, *Casablanca*. Because I'm outlining after the fact (from the completed movie) the outline will be very detailed. You can look at your watch while you're watching it and tick off the plot points and you can do the same thing for virtually every other movie! We'll see that later.

Casablanca First Act Outline

1. **Intro of Casablanca** *(One minute)*
   Opening history, info, background of time and era.

1.B. **Intro of atmosphere, politics, issues, minor characters** *(Four minutes)*
   - description/depiction of political climate
   - intro of young couple (visual)
   - intro of underground and importance of papers
   - intro of some minor running characters (pickpocket)
   - intro of Major Strasse and Col. Renault
   - verbal intro of Rick.

2. **Intro of Sam, Rick, letters of transit** *(Five minutes)*
   - intro of Rick's place as hub of planning and scheming to get away
   - intro of Sam
   - intro of workers, gambling and Rick's policies
   - intro of Rick himself and his character traits
   - intro of Ugati
   - Ugati is established as a killer while Rick is principled
   - Ugati gives Rick letters of transit (Page 10 hook).

3. **Relationships, characters, information** *(Seven minutes)*
   - Rick hides letters
   - Introduction of Ferrari (Sydney Greenstreet) and Blue Parrot
   - Yvonne and Sasha introduced
   - Rick's attitude toward women

- Relationship between Rick and Renault
- Rick's past
- Victor Laszlo talked about. (He'll want the letters of transit and he's important.)

4. **The arrest of Ugati** *(Five minutes)*
   - Renault and Strasse
   - Establish Rick as ruthless toward Ugati
   - Rick and Germans
   - More Laszlo information.

5. **Laslo appears** *(Five minutes)*
   - Laszlo and Elsa introduced
   - existence of Underground established
   - Elsa recognizes Sam, Rick.

6. **Elsa and Rick** *(Three minutes)*
   - their eyes meet, they have history
   - End of Act page 28 with three-page transition
   - Rick is drinking and for the first time, vulnerable (p. 31).

Now let's look at an outline for an unwritten movie that's a lot less detailed.

Remember my unwritten movie about Angela the Indian Activist? Here's how I'd outline that using the *Sherlock/Snitch:*

Act One

1. Angela heads a huge protest outside the reservation.
   - Intro Angela, her father and love interest.
2. She ends up in jail and is even more determined to fight the fight. (She discovers bad stuff and is punished. *(Page 10 hook.)*
3. Intro bad guys and their shenanigans. Problem gets worse *(Page 15, Inciting incident).*
4. Not sure what this is. I'll fill this "hole" with subplot (probably involving the bad guys or another character who reveals more information).
5. Another "hole" that I'll fill with subplot.
6. Angela decides to investigate situation even if it means her life is in danger *(Page 30, End Act One).*

Act Two

7. Angela's life is threatened. Love interest urges her to stop, as does her father.
8. Subplot.
9. Angela refuses to stop and goes on to investigate and discovers horrible things. *(First spike in Act Two p. 45.)*
10. Subplot.
11. Subplot.
12. She goes underground with her love interest. *(Midpoint p. 60.)*
13. They discover even more about the situation.
14. Subplot.
15. Her love interest is killed *(Second spike in Act Two p.75.)*
16. She investigates further and more dirt is dug up.
17. Subplot.
18. Her father is killed and Angela goes on the offensive to get the bad guys. *(End of Act Two p. 90.)*

Act Three

19. A trial at which Angela is triumphant.
20. Subplot tied up.
21. Angela's personal life tied up.
22. Tribe problems solved.

Notice how I've woven the subplot into the story. By outlining the structure this way, you can see where the "holes" are and where you need to put your subplot. If I just outlined according to the main plot, my script would end up being way too short. This outline technique comes in handy when you're trying to pace your film.

Remember that act three can have less than six plot points (or sometimes even more). If you end up with only twenty plot points your screenplay will end at page 110. If you've got twenty-six, it will end at page 130. Also, you don't have to know exactly how your movie ends when you start writing. You can leave your act three outline rather sketchy as long as you know how you want the issue resolved.

In this story I know I want Angela to solve the problem and be triumphant. I can worry about the machinations of the court case later on when I've got all the facts—when I come up with what she discovers and how the subplot plays out.

This outline (as un-detailed as it is) gives me the opportunity to draw from my image map/character biography. But creating that material and looking at it closely, I sometimes find a whole new story line and direction in which to take my issue-oriented movie. Perhaps, I might decide that the story of her childhood and growing sensitivity to native rights through her relationship with her father is a more compelling film than the one I was actually planning to write. I might realize that telling the story in *The Heart Tugger* (Relationship Model) is a more subtle and engaging way of drawing my audience into my issue rather than concentrating on a modern or historical incident filled with action and adventure.

For instance, I might start my movie when Angela's mother dies. This means I'd have to create a new biography of her life as a child up until that time and also a biography of her mother which I could attach to her father's biography to make a complete sub-text story. Then in writing about the father/daughter relationship, I could bring out elements in her mother and father's relationship that took root in both their biographies. Using the Relationship Model, I'd use character rather than incidents to give rise to the story.

My new plot outline would look like this:

Act One

1. Intro Angela and her mother.
2. Angela's mother dies. *(Page 10 hook.)*
3. She meets her father and is taken to the Reservation. *(Inciting incident.)*
4. Subplot.
5. Angela tries to run away but is caught. She realizes she has no choice but to stay and join in the activities.
6. She's determined not to like any of it and vows to be disruptive. *(End of Act One p. 30.)*

Act Two

7. Angela and her father. Their bad relationship continues.
8. Subplot.

9. Angela learning about and finally participating in native life. Her relationship with her father improves. *(First Spike in Act Two, Spike, p. 45.)*
10. Subplot.
11. Angela, now in Tribal college, becomes aware through her father that all is not idyllic and there are certain pressures placed upon the community that threaten it.
12. When Angela graduates, the threats become more severe and trouble comes to the Reservation threatening her father. *(Midpoint, p. 60.)*
13. Subplot.
14. Angela's relationship with her father deepens.
15. Her father encourages Angela to go to Law School to try and help her people. *(Second Spike in Act Two, p. 75.)*
16. Subplot.
17. Subplot.
18. Angela graduates in spite of continuing pressures, problems and political shenanigans. *(End of Act Two p. 90.)*

Act Three

19–24. Angela as a Native Activist resolves the issue and goes on to become a champion of her people. Her father is her best friend and supporter.

What a different film! You can see the power and importance of your model choice. It can shape your movie and even create a different direction for the film you plan to write.

Now, using Outline Magic, let's look at the social issue movie models in detail with examples of how they're used.

Social Issue Screenplay Models

In the presentation of the models, I've demonstrated how model examples are outlined specific to structure. I've done this so you can see again how the outline works and how the model is defined and played out. I'll outline one example for each model. Refer to the original template for page numbers/movie minutes and follow along while watching each film and you'll see by the time-code how each outline's plot points match structure.

The Sherlock/Snitch: Investigation/Whistleblower

This model is one that's most frequently used. Audiences like it usually because it can be written as a mystery, thriller or action/adventure while the social issue is rolled out through an investigator or whistleblower (sometimes, but not always, the same person). The audience follows the investigator/whistleblower, through a series of situations that gradually reveal and highlight the social issue.

The information about the social issue is given clearly and in order, at *specific* important points in the story (*act breaks and spikes*) and allows for lots of distinct exposition often in the form of mini-lectures. This blatant mini-lecture exposition is used either by experts, witnesses or victims to inform the investigator (and the audience) about the social issue, or by the investigator/whistleblower to inform authorities, cohorts, nay-sayers (and the audience).

The *Sherlock/Snitch* can deal with whistleblowers in a variety of ways. The whistleblower can be the person doing the investigating (as in *Silkwood*, 1983) or the investigator can use whistleblowers to further that investigation (as in *Erin Brockovich*, 2000). In that film, the main character Erin (Julia Roberts) is the ultimate investigator and through her investigation, finds whistleblowers who she joins to make a strong case against corporate greed. Sometimes (as in *The China Syndrome*, 1979) the whistleblower can even be reluctant and introduced late in the film. In *The China Syndrome*, the information is transmitted piece by piece to the audience through exposition, in a series of "discoveries." The story is a hand-off from investigators to a whistleblower through mid-point and toward the end of Act Two.

Before completely outlining *Silkwood* as a prime example of *The Sherlock/Snitch* combination, let's look more closely at *Erin Brockovich* and *The China Syndrome* as examples of alternate ways to handle whistleblowers.

EXAMPLE OF INVESTIGATOR USING WHISTLEBLOWERS

Erin Brockovich (2000)

Written by: Susannah Grant
Directed by: Steve Soderbergh
Starring: Julia Roberts and Albert Finney
Social issue: Corporate greed and public health issues.

This film is based on a true story about a real person actually named Erin Brockovich. This film fits the model because the character is an investigator who gets other people to blow whistles to bring down a huge company.

Act One is spent showing us that Erin's a feisty single mom who dresses like a hooker and thinks like a lawyer. She's tough and resilient and although she's uneducated, she wheedles her way into a job at a small law firm run by a curmudgeon (Albert Finney). *(The Inciting Incident.)*

We have lots of time to like her and understand that she's in desperate straits and will do anything to survive. That strategy is necessary to make the audience believe that she'll have the nerve and guts to get involved in something way over her head.

And that's what starts to happen at the end of *Act One* when she looks through a real-estate file and finds a suspicious toxicology report. What's blood work got to do with real estate? She asks her boss if she can investigate the file and the results of her investigation make up the rest of the movie. This is the beginning of her investigation process.

In *Act Two*, her progress is laid out in logical progression. Following an abbreviated outline template, we see how important information hits certain plot points. At plot points *7* and *8* Erin finds out that a chemical company is buying up houses on land where they've poisoned the ground water with Chromium 6. She goes to the water board and charms the yokel who runs that branch, into letting her search documents. She finds a cleanup and abatement order on waste charges of polluted groundwater and discovers that Chromium 6 does indeed cause cancer and other horrible diseases. She's away from work so long that she's fired. *(Her investigation reaps results but has consequences for her.)*

In Plot Point 9 *(First spike in Act Two)* the subplot (a saint-like love interest) kicks in. Erin gets her job back on the strength of what she's found. *(Her investigation pays off.)*

In plot points *10* and *11* Erin finds out she's got to get all the people poisoned by the Chromium to sign into a class action law suit. She meets them one by one and learns how severe their conditions are They trust her because she's down to earth and non-corporate—one of them—and they sign on to the suit. *(Her effectiveness using whistleblowers in her investigation is demonstrated.)*

At *Midpoint* (plot point *12*) Erin's got the signatures but she also gets death threats. Undeterred, she finds herself involved in one of the biggest class action lawsuits in American history. *(Dangers of whistleblowing revealed.)*

As Act Two spins out, we experience the pain of those suffering because of corporate greed and irresponsibility as Erin interviews families who have been made ill by the Chromium. We see how Erin relates to them and how she feels for them and because we identify with her, we feel as she does. We're on her side and the side of all those suffering and we agree that the corporation is horrid and evil! She smooths out wrinkles, gets more signatures and evidence to build the case.

But she spends so much time working she ignores her boyfriend and loses him. *(Investigator is effective but loses something important to her.)*

In *Act Three*, the lawsuit is won, her boyfriend comes to understand why she's worked so hard on this case and Erin winds up with $2 million—a great reward for putting herself on the line for this cause. *(Investigator is rewarded with positive results both personally and socially.)*

Throughout the film we follow Erin and get information bit by bit as the story moves. In this model Erin is an investigator who bolsters whistleblowers because, as she learns information, she brings the issue to the attention of her boss and pushes for a judicial resolution. She risks her job if she doesn't succeed and she does make a mess of her private life (the B story). She does receive threats but at least she's got the power of a law firm behind her.

Erin Brockovich demonstrates through a carefully laid out investigation, the lengths to which greedy corporations will go to cover up illegal activity even though that activity can be deadly and how little regard such corporations have for the environment in the face of a financial bottom line.

EXAMPLE OF INVESTIGATORS HANDING OFF TO A
RELUCTANT WHISTLEBLOWER

The China Syndrome (1979)

Written by: Mike Gray, T.S. Cook and James Bridges
Directed by: James Bridges
Starring: Jane Fonda, Jack Lemmon, Michael Douglas
Social Issue: Corporate greed and *public health issues (nuclear power safety)*.

Yet another corporate greed issue! Even though *The China Syndrome* focuses on nuclear power, the underlying issue is whether companies who build nuclear plants put financial concerns over public safety. This is a common, oft-repeated theme in social issue movies so we'll be seeing it again.

   The China Syndrome wasn't based on a true story or any real person—at that time! But how about this? On the evening of March 27, 1979, I watched *The China Syndrome* in its original theatrical release in a theater in Oceanside California, not far from the San Onofre nuclear plant. When my friends and I left the theater we were shaken by the possibility of meltdown but laughed it off.

   Six hours later, at 4 am on March 28, a nuclear accident occurred at the Three Mile Island Unit 2 nuclear power plant near Middletown, Pa. The details of the accident, as summarized by the U.S. National Regulatory Commission, were similar to those in the film. The NRC said that this accident was "the most serious in U.S. commercial nuclear power plant operating history."[1]

   We were amazed. "Fiction" had become fact!

   After the June 2, 2011 post-tsunami meltdown in the Fukushima nuclear facility in Japan, and the events at Chernobyl, all of us now know that these "accidents" can happen. *The China Syndrome* is still relevant today because the film demonstrates that technology is not flawless no matter how sophisticated and expensive.

Act One

1–6.   sets up Kimberly Wells (Jane Fonda) as a reporter who wants to do hard news even though she's relegated to reporting fluff pieces on the evening news. One of those light pieces is a little story on the new Ventana nuclear plant. Kim and her intrepid camera man Richard Adams (Michael Douglas) are treated to a lot of flat exposition about nuclear energy and told how it is harmless when suddenly, an ominous buzzer sounds that indicates an accident. *(Page 10 hook.)*

The PR flack taking them around tells Adams to stop shooting but, secretly, he keeps his camera running. *(Hints that reporters will investigate and whistleblow.)* The reactor crew headed by Jack Godell (Jack Lemmon)—a cool, collected professional who is clearly shaken by the incident—contains the accident and prevents core melt-down. Adams gets all the drama on tape. When Kim wants to feature the story on the news, she's told she can't. She wants to keep her job so she doesn't push it. The film's locked away in a vault. *(Potential whistleblower silenced.)*

At the end of Act One (plot point 6) Richard sneaks into the vault and steals the film. That's the set-up. We want to know if the public will find out about the accident at the plant and the ongoing danger of the nuclear site. *(Will a potential investigator/whistleblower be successful?)*

In this example, act one has fulfilled all its functions. We meet the main characters and see their determination. We are introduced to nuclear energy and the reactor. And while the first act in this example is more expository and issue oriented than the others, it still adheres to the model in that the investigation begins at the end of the act and the audience is hooked in to the main characters, and the potential danger of the issue.

The story then unfolds in act two with significant information and action at specific plot points:

Act Two

7.   Kim tells bosses she wants to do hard news and is told to keep doing fluff. *(Investigator lobbies to continue investigation.)*

8. Kim is told to get back the film Richard stole. She goes looking for him.

9. *(Spike #1 in Act Two)* Kim meets Jack Godell who is reluctant to say anything negative about the plant or nuclear power. He tells her there was no accident.

10. A worker at the plant discovers some radioactive substance. Jack knows it's serious and wants to shut down the plant to inspect it. His bosses tell him no. *(Possibility of a new whistleblower.)*

11. People are protesting nuclear energy at the NRC where Kim finds Richard and tries to get the film back for her bosses. Richard introduces her to a nuclear engineer and physics professor who tell her that she and Richard are lucky to be alive because the accident was really serious. *(Investigation moves forward.)*

12. *(Midpoint)* The China Syndrome is explained. Jack discovers that photos of the nuclear equipment have been replicated to indicate safety without testing for safety. He tells his boss and asks for new pictures and tests and is told it costs too much. He's told to back off. *(Jack becomes investigator.)*

13. The plant starts up again but Jack's conscience is bothering him. *(Motivation to whistleblow.)*

14. Jack confronts the weld checker responsible for the photos and asks for tests. He's rebuffed and says he's going to go to the NRC. He's threatened. *(Jack threatens to become whistleblower.)*

15. *(Spike #2 in Act Two)* Kim and Richard go to see Jack at home and tell him they know what happened at the plant. He confesses there's a problem. *(Jack becomes a whistleblower.)*

16. He tells them about the photos and says that the plant should be shut down, but it will cost millions. They talk about the *China Syndrome* threat. *(Whistleblower spills his guts.)*

17. Kim asks Jack to go on TV. He tells her everything and agrees to get the documents to prove his story. He tells her to send someone unrecognizable to him for the documents. *(Whistleblower is scared and fears retaliation.)*

18.   *(End of Act Two)* Jack is followed to the post office. Hector, Richard's friend and sound man, meets him there and picks up the documents. On his way to the NRC hearing where Kim plans to reveal them, he's followed, rear ended, and run off the road. (Plot point 6) It's clear that Jack has to come to the NRC to testify. *(Whistleblower knows he's in jeopardy.)*

Act Three

19–24.   The tension mounts. Jack is followed as he takes off and to avoid his pursuer, he goes to the nuclear plant where he tries to stop the start up. No one believes it when he tells them the reactor is unsafe. Upset and backed against the wall, he pulls a gun and orders everyone out. Kim and Richard rush to the scene and Kim tries to film Jack's testimony but the evil corporate bosses manage to get a swat team into the building and they gun Jack down. *(The ultimate whistleblower payback.)*

   The company workers go back to starting up the reactor when, just as Jack predicted, it begins to malfunction. Another horrible accident has to be quelled and Jack is justified.

You'll notice in this example, as in the others, that crucial information is relayed at critical plot points, but in this case, the action also plays out consistently as the whistleblower takes over from the would-be investigator who never really gets to investigate fully. You'll notice that Kim and Richard are slowly de-emphasized as Jack is brought more to the foreground.

EXAMPLE OF QUINTESSENTIAL SHERLOCK/SNITCH: INVESTIGATOR AND WHISTLEBLOWER AS THE SAME PERSON

Silkwood (1983)

Written by: Nora Ephron, Alice Arlen
Directed by: Mike Nichols
Starring: Meryl Streep, Kurt Russell and Cher
Social issue: Corporate greed, labor practices and public health issues.

Silkwood is based on a true story. The real Karen Silkwood was a worker and union representative at Kerr-McGee, an Oklahoma plutonium processing plant She blew the whistle on the company's outrageous, life-threatening procedures and died under suspicious circumstances.

This Ephron/Arlen version of events is a compelling movie full of tension and suspense. It's a great example of someone who becomes a whistleblower in the process of her investigation—that perfect blend that is *The Sherlock/Snitch*.

1. Introduction of main characters Dolly (Cher), Drew (Kurt Russell) and Karen (Meryl Streep).
   Reveal of security system at the plant and the precautions workers have to take (clothing, gloves etc.) when handling the material they work with. *(Worker safety issues introduced.)*
   Trainees visit the plant and are told about working with plutonium. Effects of radiation are minimized by supervisors. *(Corporations policy about safety issues made obvious illustrating corporate greed.)*
2. Karen asks for the weekend off. Her workers urge her to monitor herself on the way out of the work area. *(Public health issues re worker safety requirements.)*
   At lunch, workers talk about a contaminated truck that has to be somehow destroyed. Workers joke about the impossibility of getting rid of radioactive waste. *(Corporate greed re worker safety and corporate irresponsibility hinted at.)*
   Karen's relationship with co-workers explored. While she asks them to replace her on her weekend shift, an alarm goes off. It's only a test but had it been real, production would be shut down. Workers joke that the company wouldn't want to do that because it would stop production. *(Corporate irresponsibility and negligence talked about. Plant safety precautions demonstrated.)*
   A co-worker agrees to switch shifts.
3. (Inciting incident)
   When she leaves the plant at night, Karen spots some suspicious industrial sparks and notices that a truck is being worked on. She's shooed away by a supervisor. *(Corporate irresponsibility, negligence and disregard for safety hinted at.)*

Karen, Dolly and Drew take a road trip to see her kids who live with her ex-husband and his wife.

She takes the kids out and when she brings him back, her ex tells her they are all moving to Texas.

On the way home, Karen admits that she and her ex were never married and regrets not taking the kids and running off with them. Drew brings her back to earth by asking what she'd do with them. (*Second B story. The first B story is her relationship with Drew and Dolly.*)

Co-worker tells her that the truck she saw was "hot" so the company took it apart and buried it.

(*Big tip-off of corporate negligence, irresponsibility and lack of regard for safety.*)

4. Karen returns to work and finds out that the plant was shut down on the weekend because of a contamination in her section. When Karen goes to her work space everyone is wearing haz-mat masks. (*Worker safety issues.*)

    The rumor is that Karen caused the contamination because she wanted the weekend off.

5. Karen gets mad and leaves but not until her co-workers tell her to monitor herself.

    She tells Drew about the rumors. He tells her to quit her job or talk to the union about it.

    She says that the union won't care. (*Hint of union irresponsibility.*)

6. (*End of Act One*) Dolly rejects the advances of Winston, a new supervisor at the plant.

    We hear screaming and sirens. Karen's friend Thelma has been contaminated and she's brutally scrubbed down. (*Worker safety issues.*)

    Karen realizes something is seriously wrong at the plant in the way they are monitoring Thelma's condition. (*Confirmation of corporate irresponsibility re-grading worker's health.*)

7. Karen tells Thelma in front of the boss that she should have been given a nasal smear and that the company lies. (*Corporate irresponsibility re worker's safety emphasized. Hint that Karen might become a whistleblower.*)

Karen brings in a cake to celebrate a co-worker's birthday. The boss shuts down the party citing work demands and threatens job losses. Karen is told to clean up after workers leave.

8. Karen is contaminated. *(Workers safety issues again at forefront.)*

9. *(First spike in second act)* Karen reads her union manual, discovers that plutonium gives you cancer. Because she's marked as a troublemaker she gets transferred to metalography with Winston, the creepy guy who made a pass at Dolly. Karen discovers that he's doctoring the negatives of fuel rod welds to hide problems. *(Corporate negligence and purposeful disregard for safety. Karen's potential whistleblowing increases with her investigation.)*

10. Karen agrees to help the union maintain its certification at the plant.

11. The B story moves along as her female roommate Dolly (a lesbian who has professed her unrequited love for Karen) brings a girl home and has her move in.

12. *(Midpoint)* Karen goes to Washington to meet with the union and the Nuclear Regulatory Commission where she and her co-workers talk about their radiation concerns and she tells union officials about the buried contaminated truck. *(She's now officially a whistleblower.)* She gets involved with Paul Stone, one of the union officials. He and another official ask her to get documentation and she agrees.

13. Drew obliquely finds out about Karen's involvement with Paul Stone. He tells Karen to stop agitating because people will lose jobs. She tells him the *New York Times* will be involved. She refuses to quit.

14. Drew asks Karen to quit and go away with him. She refuses. He tells her he's quit. She's upset that he doesn't care that the whole plant is being poisoned. *(Revelation of her belief in the threat to workers' safety.)*

    Drew moves out because he can't take her intensity about the union investigation of the company.

    (She refuses to stop investigating and whistleblowing.)

15. Karen looks for evidence of the doctored pictures in Winston's desk. When she's discovered she makes a clever excuse.

(Danger of probing into company corruption emphasized Karen's role as an investigator.)

Union officials tell company workers about the dangers of plutonium and how lethal exposure is.

(Company's willful negligence re worker's safety emphasized.)

16. The union reveals that the company says nothing about cancer in its training literature and tells the workers there is no acceptable level of contamination. *(Company negligence and irresponsibility made plain.)*

Winston challenges Paul asking why the union didn't give them the information about cancer earlier. He believes the company will take care of him and that the union is using scare tactics to win the election. Winston is afraid that if the plant shuts down, there will be no work available in that area. *(Union irresponsibility exposed.)*

After the union wins the election, Paul Stone blows Karen off and refuses to return her messages about the mounting pressure she's under. *(Union irresponsibility reenforced.)*

17. Karen is a union rep at the plant. She and her cohorts try to negotiate with the bosses who lie to them. *(Corporate irresponsibility and corruption demonstrated.)*

18. *(End of Act Two)* Karen and Dolly talk about quitting and taking off but Karen knows she won't. She comforts Dolly whose girlfriend has just left her. Karen discovers the company has come up short on plutonium and makes notes about it. *(Company irresponsibility. Karen's whistleblowing/investigation role reinforced.)*

Her co-workers are afraid they might lose their jobs.

Karen tells Paul Stone about a worker who has been contaminated but he's not interested. He's only interested in the x-ray evidence Karen promised to get because a union negotiation is coming up. *(Union irresponsibility. Karen's investigation and whistleblowing confirmed.)*

He tells her the *New York Times* reporter is arriving.

She snoops in files and is caught by a co-worker who tells her what she's doing is dangerous. *(Karen's investigation and whistleblowing role again confirmed.)*

Her co-workers are angry and snub her when she goes to visit them in her old location.

On the way out she monitors herself and finds she's contaminated.

Act Three

19. The plant doctor tells her she's got a slight external contamination and wants her urine samples daily. On the way home, her car is hit and she's scared. It was only a deer but she's shaken.

    Drew comes back but not to move in.

20. Karen is "hot" again and the company comes in and discovers that her whole house is contaminated.

    Company workers scrape down the house removing everything. The boss accuses her of contaminating herself and the house to destroy the company. *(Corporate irresponsibility and corruption emphasized.)*

    They take Dolly away to question her.

    Karen tells her boss that someone put plutonium in her urine sample container and because she spilled the sample, her house is contaminated. *(Whistleblower has been punished by company.)*

    Karen is told that she's internally contaminated. She breaks down and tries to leave.

    Her boss tells her the company will take care of everything— give her money and a place to stay if she'll sign a document absolving them of blame. *(Corporate callous disregard for worker's health demonstrated.)*

    Karen refuses and drives off.

21. Drew comes back to the house to find it stripped. Winston shows up and Drew hits him.

    He goes home and finds Karen there. She tells him they are trying to kill her and they've contaminated her. *(Company under suspicion for evil acts. Whistleblower in danger.)*

    Drew suggests they all go to Los Alamos to be tested.

22. Karen, Drew and Dolly go to Los Alamos. On the way Karen intimates that Dolly told someone about the x-rays although she denies it. After testing, Dolly and Drew are found to be minimally contaminated but Karen is found to be distinctly

contaminated even though they insist that the contamination is still under acceptable levels.

Angry, she calls a union official and tells him to bring the *New York Times* reporter because she'll show him the documents she has. *(Determination to keep whistleblowing emphasized.)*

23. Drew talks about starting a new life, moving to Mexico and having kids with Karen. She tells him they can't have kids because she's contaminated. *(The cost of worker's safety being ignored by company.)*

24. Karen says goodbye to Drew and tells him she's going to the union meeting with the *New York Times* reporter. He asks her not to go or to fight any more. She refuses and goes to pick up the documents she's stashed with Thelma. She gets the documents and on the way to the meeting is followed by a car with blazing head-lights.

    Karen winds up off the road, her car smashed up. She's slouched over the steering wheel, and she's dead. *(The ultimate payback! Did the company kill her?)*

Pretty chilling and dramatic. The movie implies that Karen was murdered because she was a whistleblower but there has never been any proof of that in the real Karen Silkwood case. But there is good news—the plant where she worked was shut down a year after her death.

By telling the story of a courageous woman who tried to bring to light horrific corporate abuses, *Silkwood* brought to the forefront in a demonstrable and dramatic way the dangers of plutonium and the necessity for industries using it to apply rigid safety standards for their workers.

In the *Sherlock/Snitch* model, it's important to be very clear about who is telling the story and taking action. In *The China Syndrome* the investigators (a pair of reporters) are the catalysts for the whistle-blower to act. In *Erin Brockovich*, Erin's precarious financial situation and her personality was the catalyst for the investigation to start, her sense of fairness, justice and caring was the catalyst for the investigation to continue and what the investigation turned up was the catalyst for the final outcome—a lawsuit that prevailed. And in *Silkwood*, the information in the investigation she herself carried out was the catalyst for her to become the whistleblower.

The decision to investigate a situation, or to see something is wrong, usually comes at the act break around minute 30 and that's because in the *Sherlock/Snitch*, act one is usually spent getting to know the investigator/whistleblower before he/she makes a clear decision to get involved and to take action. In choosing this model, you'll need to be very clear on whether your main character is an investigator or a whistleblower or both. You'll need to draw very clear consequences for each action and make sure each piece of information is followed by a "result" or has an effect. You'll need to arrange your information and events according to specific plot points until they culminate at the end of act two propelling the film into a resolution in the third act. Notice how all three examples ratchet up the information and escalate it for impact. You'll need to do the same thing.

If you transmit that information through exposition make sure that, if it's not itself dynamic, it's followed by some dynamic implication. In *China Syndrome*, the initial exposition about how a nuclear power plant works is followed quickly by a nuclear accident that demonstrates visually and emotionally, what aspects of the plant featured in that exposition went wrong. In *Erin Brockovich*, we are told about how chemicals in drinking water cause illness, and then we are shown people who have become ill. In *Silkwood*, we are told about the possibility of contamination from plutonium and then we see what happens when someone is contaminated. We should get information and then be blown away by its implications.

Other examples of *The Sherlock/Snitch* and their social issues:

Missing (1982): A father looking for his missing son in Chile uncovers political corruption: Abuse of (government) power and of course political corruption.

The Insider (1999): A whistleblower working for "Big Tobacco" uncovers its flagrant disregard for public health: Corporate greed, public health.

North Country (2005): A woman miner endures horrible abuse and wins a lawsuit: Women's rights (sexual harassment).

The Whistleblower (2010): An American cop in Bosnia uncovers U.N. Peacekeepers' complicity in human rights (sex trafficking): international political corruption.

Exercise

Come up with another example of *The Sherlock/Snitch* and outline it.

The Chuckle: The Satirical Model

I call this model *The Chuckle* because written as a straight-up comedy (genre) it can lead to giant chuckles and written as a dark satirical piece it will still brings forth a "chuckle" of understanding and awareness. It's an exceptionally popular model and that's because when people are laughing, and/or amused, they relax and when they relax, they're more susceptible to messages.

However, please know that just because characters have funny dialogue, doesn't always mean that *The Chuckle* is in play. *Good Morning Vietnam* has some hilarious lines and scenes thanks to Robin Williams, but it's an example of *The Shining Knight* because his character heroically and at great personal expense, takes on the army to expose censorship. And the fact that it's a true story takes it out of the satirical model because it really happened. No send up here. It was the unvarnished truth just amped up for audience delight.

As I've already pointed out, *The Chuckle has* had great success in getting social issues across to audiences. Historically, people have always made fun of leaders and situations. The greatest comedies have lots to say about society and stand-ups like George Carlin and his ilk have made fortunes with their funny rants about society and its foibles.

But beware—if you choose this model, you've got to be careful that your humor doesn't cross the line. There are some things you really shouldn't make fun of because they're far too serious. It's difficult, for instance, to see the lighter side of genocide. And it's not easy to laugh at cruelty or injustice. If you do that, you will turn audiences off.

That doesn't mean you can't be outrageous, dark or caustic. *Monty Python* was really bold and wacky and did some pretty insane things, but people still laughed. And I don't mean that you should avoid controversy. I *do* mean that you shouldn't come across as an insensitive unfeeling boor by making fun of a social issue that isn't funny.

The idea is that you should boldly make a statement and then reinforce it by incident upon hilarious incident until the audience gets your point. It's not so much jokes but the absurdity of the building incidents that make this model. Remember—the incidents don't have to be funny at all. They can be ironic or dark. They just need to make your point in a startling way.

Wag The Dog (1997)

Written by: Hillary Henkin and David Mamet
Directed by: Barry Levninson
Starring: Dustin Hoffman and Robert De Niro
Social issue: Political corruption and abuse of power (by media).

I've used *Wag the Dog* as an example because it's funny, but it also delivers a dark message. This film demonstrates through a series of absurd and very funny sequences, how corrupt politicians, to serve their own purposes, use the media to distort, manipulate and even fabricate world events.

Here are the plot points so you can see how the satirical situation with regard to the social issue evolves within the screenplay structure.

Act One

1. With a mere 14 days to go before the election, the President is caught in a sexual scandal with an underage girl. He hires super-fixer Conrad Brean (Robert De Niro) to hush things up. *(Intro political cover-up of an amusing scandal.)*

2. Brean determines that a crisis must be created to divert attention from the scandal—perhaps a war with Albania. *(Page 10 Hook: Manipulation introduced. The idea seems ludicrous and sketchy.)*

3. *(Inciting incident.)* Brean goes to Hollywood to hire Producer Stanley Motss (Dustin Hoffman) to fabricate a war. He tells Stanley he can NEVER tell anyone about what he did. He can never ever talk about it. Stanley agrees. *(Process of manipulation by media begins.)*

4. Motss hires a song writer (Willie Nelson) and a "fad king" to help him come up with a reason for the war (Albanians have a suitcase nuclear bomb) and some commercial products related to it.
    (Details of process of manipulation. Hiring creative types to promote a war is ironic.)

5. Motss sets up music and product placement and figures out news footage. They decide to say "the president is *going* to war with Albania"—not *"declaring* war." (A real bit of satire here on the U.S. military actions that don't actually declare war.)
    (Political corruption and media manipulation join forces in an amusing way.)

6. *(End of Act One)* Motss and his crew are in the studio (with the President's approval and input—he wants an escaping Albanian girl to hold a *white* kitten rather than a calico) and the "news footage" airs. *(The President is in on it. Corruption at the highest levels. Hilarious nit-picking emphasizing detail over substance.)*

Act Two

7. After congratulating themselves on their achievement Brean and Motss are stopped and questioned by the CIA. *(Forces trying to uncover political corruption and media manipulation introduced.)*

8. They convince the CIA agent (William Macey) that there is a war against terrorism. (Ironically this was well before 2011!) Great line: "There is a war because I'm watching it on MTV!" *(Power of media to convince opposition.)*

9. *(First spike in Act Two)* The President's plane is diverted to Boca Raton so he can land in the rain (for effect) and give his coat to the grandmother of an Albanian girl who's presenting him with "something ceremonial." A wonderful *We Are The World-like* theme song for the war *(We Guard Our American Borders)* is rehearsed in the studio but in mid-song, the CIA announces that the Albanian situation has been resolved. *(Opposition uses media's own tactics to manipulate agenda.)*

10. Motss repeats his mantra: "This is nothing!" He compares this problem to a show business glitch he's experienced in the past. This becomes a running gag. To counteract the C.I.A.'s putting an end to the war, Motss and the fad king come up with the idea that there's a soldier still behind "enemy lines" who's been captured by the Albanians. They make up a new song based on an icon they think will "sell"—a shoe! They find a soldier whose name has "shoe" in it, as their poster boy. *(Lengths to which manipulators will go. Hilarious grasping-at-straws solution which, though far-fetched, works.)*

11. Motss writes a speech for the president to deliver about "old shoe," William Schuman. He refuses to deliver it. *(President balks at personally delivering a lying manipulation.)*

12. *(Midpoint)* Motss assembles a bunch of secretaries in the Oval Office and delivers the speech to them with the President watching in the shadows. It's a tear jerker and the President agrees to give the speech. It's announced that a man is missing behind enemy lines and his image is photo-shopped to look like his captors have videotaped him, wearing a ratty sweater he's unraveled to send a message in Morse Code. The message "Courage Mom" becomes a hit song. *(Manipulators' power to convince is reinforced. Political corruption at highest level is reinforced. Implausible hilarious solution bought by public.)*

13. Motss and Brean hang shoes all over town to keep people thinking about "Old Shoe." They have their songwriter come up with what sounds like an old blues song about an old shoe and sneak it into the Library of Congress. They begin to create a memorial for the Albanian conflict and create "old shoe" merchandising. *(Manipulators reinforce their message with artifacts.)*

14. They get one of their staffers to plant the idea of the "old" record in the mind of a reporter by sleeping with him. The song catches on and plans are made to find a soldier whose name's got "shoe" in it and stage a fake rescue/homecoming *(Lengths to which manipulators will go to get their message out are reinforced and their ability to succeed is amazing.)*

15. *(Second spike in Act Two)* Schumann (Woody Harrelson) arrives on the plane taking everyone to a staged arrival. It turns out he's a wacked-out convict who has spent the last twelve years in jail for raping a nun. They've got to come up with something, but they figure they can say he's lost his mind because he's been through a lot. *(Manipulators are very resourceful in the face of a funny problem.)*

16. The plane crashes in a storm. (Motss: "This is nothing!") They all hitch a ride on a Harvester (driven by an illegal immigrant) to a small store in the middle of nowhere. Brean calls to have the event surrounding their arrival delayed. *(Manipulators are resourceful and remain confident in the face of adversity.)*

17. Meanwhile, Schumann attacks the store owner's wife. The store owner gets a gun and shoots Schumann. (Motss: "This is nothing!") *(Manipulators remain undaunted in the face of even funnier adversity.)*

18. *(End of Act Two)* Schumann is dead and they send his coffin home. They orchestrate a grand homecoming for a fallen hero (complete with bereaved dog). The President is re-elected. *(The manipulators are victorious.)*

Act Three

19. The credit for the President's re-election is given to a terrible "Don't Change Horses In Mid-Stream" commercial. Stanley freaks out. He wants credit because he never gets any. There is no Academy Award for producing. He says "It's the best work I've ever done in my life because it's so honest!" *(Manipulators take pride in their work and see nothing wrong with supporting political corruption.)*

20. Brean warns Stanley he had promised to never talk about what he did. Stanley refuses to listen. He leaves saying he'll get credit no matter what. Brean gives some government handlers a nod.
   (Corrupt politicians will go to any lengths to protect themselves.)

21. The Harvester driver is secretly sworn in as a citizen so the President doesn't have to fear the "hire an illegal alien" scandal.

Stanley's death is announced as a pool-side heart-attack. *(Corrupt politicians will betray even those who have helped them in desperate attempt to hold power.)*

A news break announces that Albanian terrorists have a bomb! *(In the end, media can be powerful enough to create real situations out of fantasies.)*

It's obvious in this example how the situation keeps on spiraling into more and more absurdity. There are hilarious lines galore in this movie but they are tinged with irony. Based on the international turmoil we've all seen since the film was released in the late 1990s, audiences are left to wonder how current events are influenced by politicians who are up for re-election.

Other examples of *The Chuckle* and their social issues:

The Great Dictator (1940): Charlie Chaplin spoofs Hitler (War issues.)

The Mouse That Roared (1959): A minuscule country goes to war with the U.S. (War issues.)

Dr. Strangelove (1964): Wacky governments play with nuclear attacks. (War issues.)

A Clockwork Orange (1971): Aversion therapy to solve a national crime problem goes horribly wrong. (Criminal justice re violence and social decay.)

Network (1976): A TV station uses a disturbed anchorman to promote itself. (Abuse of power by the media.)

Brazil (1985): The effects of an increasing "Big Brother" society. (Political corruption.)

War of the Roses (1989): A couple goes at it in a contentious divorce. (Breakup of the family re divorce.)

Bob Roberts (1992): A folk-singer runs a corrupt election campaign. (Political corruption.)

The Hudsucker Proxy (1994): A huge company plans a scam. (Corporate greed.)

I had to stop myself from giving even more examples of this model. I told you it was popular!

Exercise

Come up with another example of *The Chuckle* and outline it.

The Lawyer-Up: The Trial Model

If you chose *The Lawyer-Up*, you'll need to do a considerable amount of legal research to get your facts straight and to be authentic in courtroom procedures, particularly if your entire film takes place in the courtroom. You'll need to know legal language and understand the intricacies of your case. That's why most films in this model are based on true stories where the screenwriter can draw from actual trials or from novels by writers (John Grisham etc.) who have already done the research. This is another really popular model because it lends itself to exposing egregious transgressions in a systematic and clear way and stipulates punishment in the form of verdicts. Audiences love to see social issue crimes punished!

In the following example, notice how the lawyers gather evidence and how much time is spent discussing and working out the case. Even though there is investigation involved (as in *The Sherlock/Snitch*), and whistleblowers might be used, this model revolves around lawyers who are the stars of this show and specifically their acumen in the trial process. This model is usually as much about the lawyer as it is about the social issue.

A Few Good Men (1992)

Written by: Aaron Sorkin
Directed by: Rob Reiner
Starring: Tom Cruise, Jack Nicholson, Demi Moore
Social issue: Abuse of power (by the military) and criminal justice issues.

A Navy lawyer (Lt. Daniel Kafee played by Tom Cruise) finds himself assigned to the case of two Guantanamo Bay marines charged with murder in a Code Red gone wrong. The marines claim the Code Red—an illegal hazing of enlisted men by their peers as a punishment for perceived infractions in the Marine Code—was ordered by their superior officers. The officers claim that they didn't order it.

The military expects that the two men charged will plea bargain their way into a relatively short sentence and the whole thing will be forgotten. That's why they appoint Lt. Daniel Kafee (Tom Cruise) to defend the men. He's a master of the plea bargain and has never gone to court.

At first Kafee doesn't bother to prepare the case and simply jumps on a quick plea deal but as the evidence unfolds and he's egged on by Lt. Cmdr Joanne Galloway (Demi Moore) who's been on the case from the beginning, he starts to see that perhaps the men do need to go to trial.

Here's how the events play out in the model:

Act One

1. The Code Red event takes place against Private William Santiago. *(Opening hook.)*
   Intro Lt. Cmdr Holloway. She expects to be given the case but her superiors refuse to let her have it. *(Visual of abuse and introduction of legal action.)*
2. Intro Lt. Kaffe. He's a casual baseball-addicted guy who is irreverent and thrilled by his own ability. He gets a plea deal with no effort and it's obvious he's a whiz at that. *(Introduction of possibility of legal expediency by someone who's an expert at it.)*
3. *(Inciting incident)* Kaffe and Galloway meet. It's not pleasant. Galloway warns him she's responsible for seeing he does his job. *(The necessity for legal justice emphasized.)*
4. Flashback before the Code Red incident. Intro. Col. Nathan R. Jessup (Jack Nicholson).
   Jessup is mean and "take-no-prisoners" tough. He knows that Santiago, the Code Red victim, has written fourteen letters requesting a transfer and that in his last letter, he threatened to name a soldier who was involved in an illegal shooting incident at the Guantanamo base. Jessup's long-time friend, Lt. Col. Markinson, suggests Santiago be transferred. Jessup refuses and instead insists that Santiago be "trained." He orders Lt. John Kendrick (Kiefer Sutherland) to make sure it's done. *(Introduction of unfeeling military official who exerts unreasonable power in spite of requests that he should not.)*
5. The defendants, Lance Cpl. Harold Dawson (Wolfgang Bodison) and PFC Louden Downey (James Marshall) arrive

in Washington and are locked up. Galloway tells Kaffe she wants him off the case. He tells her to shove it. *(Indications that squabbles may hamper legal justice.)*

6. *(End of Act One)* Kaffe meets the defendants who explain Code Red is a disciplinary action. They say they put a rag in Santiago's mouth, taped his arms and legs and were going to shave his head when they saw blood and called an ambulance. Although the prosecution maintains the rag contained poison, Dawson denies that. He gives an impassioned speech about the Marine Code and honor but refuses to say much else. Kaffe blows up and tells Dawson to realize "I'm the only friend you got!" *(Assertion of the potential efficacy of legal justice.)*

Act Two

7. The prosecutor (Kevin Bacon) offers a plea deal of twelve years in prison. He also says that Kendrick told all the Marines not to touch Santiago. Kaffe thinks it is strange Kendrick's name was brought up.

    Jo comes to make peace and tell Kafee that she's spoken to the prisoners. Kaffe berates her for seeing his defendants but she says she got authorization from Downey's aunt to speak to him. *(Squabbles again threaten to undermine legal justice process.)*

8. Kaffe, his assistant Lt. Sam Weinberg (Kevin Pollack) and Galloway go to Guantanamo. They meet Kendrick and Nicholson who remembers Kaffe's late father—a famous lawyer who was once Secretary of State. They inspect Santiago's room. Kendrick tells them Santiago is dead because he had no code of honor. They have lunch. *(Military power and hubris is demonstrated.)*

9. *(First spike in Second Act)* At the lunch, Jessup lies and says he was going to transfer Santiago and that he was scheduled to take the first plane out of Guantanamo at 6am the following morning. Kaffe asks for a copy of the transfer order. Jessup agrees to give it to him. When Galloway asks Jessup about Code Red, he says he knows it is illegal (his on-the-record comment) but off the record, he says he encourages it. The

lunch ends with Jessup dressing down both Galloway and Kaffe. *(Military power and hubris reenforced.)*

10. Markinson disappears. Galloway tells Kaffe she's Downey's attorney (his aunt hired her) and she thinks Kendrick ordered the Code Red because the defendants said he did. They said that after the initial platoon meeting where he told people to lay off Santiago, he met privately with Dawson and Downey and ordered them to do a Code Red on Santiago. She refuses a new plea deal (two years) and wants the trial to go to court. She argues with Kaffe. *(More threat to legal justice from squabbles.)*

11. The defendants refuse the deal too. Kaffe blows up but Dawson makes an impassioned plea about honor. Kaffe thinks about what Dawson said.

12. *(Midpoint)* Kaffe's late for court and when he arrives he refuses the plea deal and pleads not guilty. *(Legal justice process begins.)*

13. The team outlines the defense. They look for Markinson. Galloway and Kaffe make up. *(Legal justice process assured because squabbles are over.)*

14. The first day of trial. In opening statements, the prosecution says the defendants committed murder. The defense contends they were following orders.

15. *(Second spike in Act Two)* Kendrick testifies he told his men not to touch Santiago. The military staff doctor gives testimony that Santiago died from lactic acidosis because he was poisoned, even though no traces of poison were found in his system. Kaffe asks if Santiago could have had another medical condition that could have caused acidosis.
The doctor admits he put Santiago on restricted duty because of symptoms that were emblematic of a heart condition. *(Power of military to cover up and obfuscate.)*

16. Doctor refuses to change his testimony and clings to the poison theory. He doesn't want to admit he might have made a medical mistake. *(Military not willing to admit mistakes.)*

17. Galloway asks Kaffe out to dinner. They "bond." She tells him she thinks he's an exceptional lawyer. He tells her they are going to lose.

18. *(End of Act Two)* Markinson suddenly appears and offers to help Kaffe. He tells Kaffe that Kendrick ordered the Code Red and that Santiago was never going to be transferred. He signed the transfer order five days after Kaffe asked for it. He also says that there was an 11pm flight out of Guantanamo besides the 6am flight Jessup cited. Kafee tells the prosecutor about Markinson who says Markinson is nuts and warns Kaffe if he accuses senior officers of illegal activities without evidence, he will be court marshaled. *(Military power versus legal justice clearly defined.)*

Act Three

19. Kendrick denies he ordered Code Red during testimony. *(An officer covers up.)*
20. It becomes obvious that Jessup, through big-time connections, fixed the flight log book to make it look like there were no earlier flights out of Guantanamo. *(Top officer covers up.)*
21. Downey testifies that he was given the Code Red order by Dawson.
     Markinson shoots himself.
     Kafee gets drunk in despair that they will lose the case. *(Legal justice in jeopardy because of death of whistleblower and admission of defendant.)*
22. Kaffe decides to put Jessup on the stand and brings in two Air Force people to sit in the court room as potential witnesses that the flight log was doctored.
23. Kaffee confronts Jessup aggressively, and finally takes the ultimate step and accuses him of ordering the Code Red. In spiraling anger and egotism, Jessup finally admits he did order it and that he'd do it again! *(Military abuse of power admitted.)*
24. Jessup is arrested, and the defendants are freed on all the charges except for conduct unbecoming a marine. They are given a dishonorable discharge–something Dawson always dreaded. But in the end Dawson realizes that he was wrong to follow the Code Red order because as a marine, he needed to protect and not punish the weak. *(Military abuse of power punished and legal justice delivered.)*

As is often the case in *The Lawyer-Up*, the first act is spent describing the circumstances of the case and introducing the lawyer(s). Sometimes, as in *A Few Good Men*, they "fight" over the case and sometimes, the lawyer doesn't even want the case and has to be convinced to take it. By the end of act one, those issues usually get resolved and the process of gathering evidence begins.

Notice that in this example we don't get into the courtroom until the middle of the movie. In this model it isn't necessary to stay in the courtroom. Of course you can do that but as the outline demonstrates, scenes outside the courtroom can establish evidence, solve problems and reveal courtroom strategy. Then the courtroom scenes can be used to show the effectiveness of that evidence, problem solving and strategy. And in these courtroom scenes—and certainly in the third act, everything builds to the final outcome—getting the guilty to admit their guilt in the trial.

In *A Few Good Men* Jessup's "admission" in the form of a rant (although he didn't consider himself guilty of anything) brought to mind Lt. Cmdr Philip Francis Queeg's rant (Humphrey Bogart) in *The Caine Mutiny* (1954). Jessup's rant was in favor of honor, country and military while Queeg's rant about missing strawberries was the escalating babble of a madman. The audience knows Jessup isn't mad. He's just got a point of view that's narrow and nasty, giving voice to exactly what this movie is all about—the abuse of military power in the name of order and a twisted idea of patriotism. The fact that Jessup was set up to admit what he did, makes the statement that eventually military abuse of power will be exposed and punished.

Other examples of *The Lawyer-Up* and their social issues:

Inherit the Wind (1960): The trial of a science teacher arrested for teaching evolution (censorship).

Judgment at Nuremberg (1961): An American Court tries Nazis for war crimes (genocide).

To Kill a Mockingbird (1962): A southern lawyer defends a black man on a rape charge (racism).

The Verdict (1982): An alcoholic lawyer takes a malpractice suit to trial (addiction re alcoholism, and corporate greed re medical malpractice).

The Rain Maker (1997): A young lawyer learns how devious the law can be (criminal justice).

Runaway Jury (2003): Manipulation of a court trial (criminal justice).

Exercise

Come up with another *Lawyer-Up* and outline it.

The Life: The Biopic Model

This model tells someone's life story and demonstrates how a social issue is woven through it.

These stories can be about famous people or they can be about "ordinary" folks but in both cases, this model covers a lot of ground. The audience gets to know the main character over a long sweep of years. You can tell the story in a linear way, starting with childhood or a point near there, or you can skip around using flashbacks but the movie as a whole will give the audience a clear picture of how the social issue affected the life of the principal character.

This model can be tricky because crucial life events may not be attached to the social issue and that means that not all structural hit points (midpoints, spikes, even act breaks) would involve the social issue. Just make sure that the points involving the social issue are frequent enough to warrant calling this a social issue movie. For example, if the character is a drug addict and overcomes that, this may be the central theme in his life and so it fits the model.

If, for example, we were writing a biopic about Robert Mitchum, and if, as he actually did, he went to a party, smoked a joint and was arrested and then continued on in his life with nothing more involving drugs, the movie wouldn't fit *That's Life*. In fact, it wouldn't be a social issue film at all.

The social issue needs to be ongoing and significant.

A Beautiful Mind (2001)

Written by: Akiva Goldsman
Directed by: Ron Howard
Starring: Russell Crowe, Ed Harris, Jennifer Connelly
Social issue: Mental health.

This is the life story of a real person—Nobel Prize winner John Nash—who suffers from schizophrenia but learns how to minimize the hallucinations that go with it so he can go on to have a productive life. Akiva Goldsman got an Academy Award for best Adapted Screenplay for the film which won Best Picture of the Year. Russell Crowe got a nomination for his performance which was brilliant because he was able to play a genius in the throes of mental illness.

The film is so effective because it demonstrates, from the point of view of the person afflicted with hallucinations, just how real they can be. From the beginning of the film the audience takes for granted that John Nash's world is real and it isn't until later in the film that it becomes clear this reality isn't solid. In the breakdown of plot points we can see where the social issue enters the story and how powerfully it does so.

Act One

1. Intro John Nash at Princeton. He meets his classmates (we learn from them that he's a mathematical whiz) and his roommate Charles. *(Sense that main character is odd and quirky.)*

2. It's obvious that Nash doesn't like people and they don't like him. His roommate tries to loosen him up but Nash says he's there to work. His goal is to find an original idea. He doesn't go to class. When he's challenged to a chess game by one of his classmates, he's certain he'll win and brags a lot. When he loses he's surprised and confounded. *(Main character acts strangely and inappropriately.)*

3. Nash still hasn't found a topic for his thesis. He's not eating. His room-mate gets him to go out to a bar where he sees a girl he finds attractive. He jumps right in and asks her to have "intercourse" with him. She slaps him and leaves, further cementing our opinion of him as a weirdo.

   His professor tells him he's not doing well enough to be recommended for any post-grad work—that he's got to think in terms of accomplishment and not recognition which it's obvious he's after. *(Main character is troubled and thwarted.)*

4. Nash is broken up about the professor's comments and freaks out. His roommate calms him and encourages him. They throw his desk out the window together.

Nash goes back to the bar and the girl who slapped him shows up with her friends. There is an attraction but all the other guys want her too. He puts forth a theory of how to approach her, gets an idea and leaves quickly. *(Main character is impulsive.)*

5. He is inspired to make more calculations and finally hands a paper in to his professor who says it flies in the face of economic theory but that it is a breakthrough that will assure him any placement he wants. *(Main character's behavior and attitude is vindicated by his success.)*

6. *(End of Act One)* Five years later, the pentagon calls Nash in to decipher code from Moscow. He does the calculations in his head, sees patterns in the lists of numbers and figures out the code. It's a set of geographical coordinates in the States. He's escorted out of the building but not before he sees a man in a black hat and trench coat watching him. When he goes back to the institute where he's set to teach, we find out he's made the cover of *Fortune* magazine. He's upset because he wasn't pictured on the cover by himself and reluctantly goes to teach a class where he's contemptuous of his students.
One of his female students interests him. *(Main character is involved in unusual circumstances, demonstrates unusual abilities and flagrant egotism.)*

Act Two

7. Nash meets with William Parcher (Ed Harris), the man in the black hat. Parcher tells him he's from the Department of Defense and takes Nash to a secret warehouse where covert activities take place. He's given a higher security clearance and told the Soviets have the atomic bomb and that they are going to detonate it in the U.S. Parcher tells Nash there are sleeper agents in the U.S. who communicate in codes. Parcher flatters Nash by telling him he's the most gifted code breaker ever and gives him an assignment to scan periodicals and decipher their codes. A radium diode with an access code is implanted into Nash's arm to give him access to the drop box where he must deliver the deciphered documents. *(Main character submits to unusual procedures to succeed.)*

Alicia (Jennifer Connelly), the girl from his class, shows up and asks him to dinner. He agrees.

8. Alicia and Nash go to a fancy party where they get close. He shows her patterns in stars but realizes, when they are out in the garden, that he is being watched by Parcher. He begins his assignment reading newspaper clippings and sees code embedded there. *(Main character demonstrates unusual abilities again.)*

9. *(First spike in Act Two)* Nash makes his first drop. He places his implanted arm under a box. Numbers light up and a gate opens into the yard of a huge mansion. He places an envelope into a letter box but gets frightened when he sees a black car watching him. *(Main character is suspicious and fearful.)*

10. He goes on another date with Alicia but can't make small talk. He says that all he really wants to do is have "intercourse" with her as soon as possible. She kisses him and we assume she's on board with that.

   He is in the throes of deciphering more code in magazines when his roommate Charles shows up and brings his small niece with him. He tells Nash that he's now at Harvard and that his sister (the girl's mother) died so he took her in. Nash takes a shine to the girl and he's especially glad to see Charles after all these years. He tells him about Alicia.

11. Nash is late for his date with Alicia but tries to appease her by giving her a birthday gift of a multi-faceted crystal. He asks her for a proof of her commitment to him and she says you can't prove love. He asks her to marry him.

   They marry and Nash is nervous when he sees Parcher watching their wedding. *(Main character seems paranoid and frightened.)*

12. Nash makes another drop. After he's done that, Parcher pulls up in a black car and tells Nash they are being followed. Nash gets in the car. They are shot at and side-swiped. Nash is terrified but won't accept Parcher's offer of a gun. Parcher shoots the men following them and they careen off a pier into the river. *(Main character is terrified.)*

13.   *(Midpoint)* He comes home but won't tell Alicia where he was. He's freaked out and closes himself away from her. He won't talk to her. He goes to class but can't continue because he keeps looking out the window searching for cars that he thinks are coming for him. *(Main character is paranoid.)*
      He loses it and leaves class. Parcher calms him down.
      Alicia tells him she's pregnant.

14.   Parcher tells him that attachments are bad for him. Nash wants to quit the assignment. Parcher says that he'll tell the Russians and they will kill Nash.
      He goes home and tells Alicia to leave. He sees cars outside his house watching him. Alicia realizes something is wrong but she leaves. *(Main character's paranoia escalates and his behavior is noticed by his wife.)*

15.   Nash goes to Harvard to deliver a lecture and runs into Charles. He asks Charles for help.
      As Nash is delivering his lecture, he sees men in suits watching him. He's convinced it's the Russians and runs away in the middle of the lecture. The men catch up with him and tackle him to the ground. *(Main character's paranoia is out of control.)*
      One of them says he's Dr. Rosen (Christopher Plummer) a psychiatrist but Nash doesn't believe him and punches him in the face. The man gives Nash a shot and he passes out. *(Main character's illness confronted but we're still not sure.)*

16.   *(Second spike in Act Two).* Nash wakes up shackled to a chair in Dr. Rosen's office. He tries to wriggle out of his restraints but finds himself on the floor. He sees Charles sitting in a corner weeping. He's convinced that Charles betrayed him. Dr. Rosen tells him there's no one there.
      Rosen tells Alicia that Nash is schizophrenic and paranoid and that he has hallucinations. He convinces her that Charles is imaginary.
      Rosen wants Alicia to find out about Nash's work which she believes is classified.
      She goes to his office at the Institute and sees his walls papered with magazines and numbers.

She goes to the drop box and finds that the mansion (which we saw as grand) is dilapidated and that the supposed drop box is just an old mail box. She opens it. *(Main character's mental illness exposed and defined.)*

16. She visits Nash in the hospital. He apologizes for acting crazy and he sounds quite "normal" until he tells Alicia that people might be listening in to their conversation. He promises to tell her everything about his work. He wants her to help him get out. As he tells her about his "assignment" for the government, she tells him that one of his friends followed him to his drop box. She pulls out all the envelopes he's been stuffing in there. They're unopened. She tells him that everything is in his mind and that he's sick. He can't believe her and freaks out. *(Main character confronted by the facts of his illness and refuses to accept them.)*

17. He slits his arm looking for his implant and believes it's been removed.

    He gets shock therapy as Alicia watches. Dr. Rosen says he's got to go through it five times a week for ten weeks. *(Treatment of mental illness detailed.)*

    Time passes. Alicia has her baby. The delusions have passed. A Princeton friend from the past comes to visit. Nash makes jokes about his state of mind. He tells his friend the pills he's taking make it hard for him to do his work.

    The friend looks at Nash's current project. It's gobbledy-gook.

    The pills make him unable to relate to his baby and ultimately to Alicia. She has a screaming fit when he rejects her sexual advance and feels despair. He is thoughtful and upset. *(Main character is debilitated by his medication.)*

18. *(End of Act Two)* He stops taking his pills. He starts seeing patterns again. The delusions are back.

    He takes over a small shack at the back of his house.

    Alicia leaves him inside with the baby and goes to hang up clothes. She hears a radio playing in the shack and finds it's all filled with paper and codes. Realizing he's got the baby, she runs into the house and rescues the baby from a bath nearly filled with water. Nash tells her not to worry because Charles is watching the baby.

They fight. Parcher appears and tells Nash to get rid of Alicia. Nash refuses. Parcher pulls a gun and is about to fire when Nash lunges at him. Alicia is knocked down. *(Main character's mental illness returns and is demonstrated.)*

She calls Dr. Rosen, leaves the house and gets into her car. Nash runs out of the house and jumps on the car hood to stop her.

He tells her that he's realized Charles can't be real because the niece he sees always with him, never gets older. *(Main character accepts his illness.)*

Act Three

19. Nash admits to Dr. Rosen that he's still seeing Charles and his niece. He says he stopped his meds because he couldn't function. Rosen says he'll increase or change the meds. Nash says he'll apply his mind to stop the delusions. He's told that without treatment, the fantasies will take over again. Nash doesn't want to go back to the hospital because he fears he won't come home again. Alicia tells him that Dr. Rosen told her to sign commitment papers if he didn't go willingly. He pleads with her to let him work it out on his own and she should leave for her own safety. Alicia sends Rosen away and stays. *(Main character determines to get control of his mental illness and is supported by his wife.)*

20. Two months later, Nash goes back to Princeton to see one of his old friends who is now a department head. Charles appears and Nash tries to ignore him. He confronts Charles publically. A crowd gathers. Nash realizes he looks as if he's talking to himself. He's embarrassed and flees.

He comes home and tells Alicia that he's considering going to the hospital again. She encourages him and tells him to try harder. *(Main character confronts his hallucinations and is discouraged but his wife bucks him up.)*

21. Nash goes back to Princeton. He says goodbye to Charles and his niece and says he won't be talking to them ever again.

They are still there and he consistently ignores them. *(Main character takes definitive action and resolves to ignore his hallucinations. He acts on this.)*

22. Students make fun of him because of his strange demeanor. He's solving a math problem on the window of the library when a student approaches him to get an opinion on work. Soon, he's holding impromptu seminars in the library. He tells his department head that he wants to teach. *(Main character makes the successful effort to go on with his life in spite of his mental illness.)*

23. He's begun teaching again when a man appears and tells him he's being considered for the Nobel Prize. His colleagues present him with much coveted special pens for this accomplishment. *(Main character achieves success and public respect in spite of his illness.)*

24. He receives the Nobel and makes a speech thanking his wife. He's still ignoring his visions but now he's enjoying his success and his life.

This film runs 135 minutes so some of the page counts in the plot points have been elongated. That is because some of the plot points take up more pages than the standards described earlier but notice that the structure points are still emphasized.

A Beautiful Mind was written so that the audience doesn't realize Nash is mentally ill until the second spike in act two. We certainly get the idea that Nash is agitated and paranoid but it comes as a surprise that Charles and Parcher aren't real and that none of his spy activity has been. This is a very compelling way of involving the audience in the social issue because it can actually experience to some extent, what it means to have delusions and just how real these delusions can be. Charles and Parcher and their actions certainly seem real—especially in a movie sense. And that's perhaps why a film like this can demonstrate the power schizophrenia has over a character much better than a book can. When the audience buys into the experience of the character, it also buys into his point of view, and life experiences and later, when the audience discovers that point of view is warped, and that those life experiences may have been bogus, it's chilling. That's why *A Beautiful Mind* is a great example of *The Life*: The Biopic Model dealing with a social issue.

Here are some other examples of *The Life and* their social issues:

Lady Sings The Blues (1972): The life of blues singer Billie Holiday whose life was destroyed by addiction (addiction re drugs).

Gandhi (1982): The career of Gandhi and his fight for Indian Independence using the principles of non-violence (peace issues).

My Left Foot (1989): The story of Christy Brown who was born with cerebral palsy. Using only his left foot, he learned to paint and write (disabilities).

What's Love Got To Do With It (1993): The life of Tina Turner who broke away from her abusive singing partner/husband to achieve personal stardom (domestic abuse).

Ray (2004): The life of Ray Charles, a man who achieved stardom in spite of his blindness and brush with addiction (disabilities and addiction re drugs).

Milk (2008): The life and times of gay activist Harvey Milk, America's first openly gay elected official who fought for gay rights and was assassinated (gay issues).

Exercise

Come up with another *The Life* movie and outline it.

The Heart-Tugger: The Relationship Model

The Heart-Tugger is all about drama and feeling. Movies in this model are designed to tug on audience's emotions and they make their point by pushing certain "heart" buttons to make viewers actually feel the impact of the social issue. Some of the relationships explored in this model are warm and fuzzy, but they can also be dysfunctional and chaotic putting characters in turmoil and creating a great deal of angst. This model needs to frame the social issue in ways that are deeply personal to each of the characters and while doing that, demonstrate how their behavior is affected and their lives changed.

The Squid and the Whale is a movie just like that. It's shorter than most movies—at only 81 minutes it even beats the 90-minute film at structure modification so its outline, with regard to structural points, will be different from the ones which we've already seen.

The Squid and the Whale (2005)

Written and directed by: Noah Baumback
Starring: Jeff Daniels, Laura Linney, Jesse Eisenberg
Social issue: Breakdown of the family (separation and divorce).

This film is all about how characters behave toward each other during a separation and divorce. It demonstrates how parents use children and how children, in spite of trying to resist being used, end up falling for parental "seduction." It also points out the absolute alienation and disharmony children feel when their parents split up. It's interesting that tennis and ping pong are featured so prominently in this film because those games are really a metaphor for how the parents interact with their children. They serve up examples of dysfunction and get dysfunctional behavior thrown back at them.

Act One

1. The family plays tennis together. Bernard, the father (Jeff Daniels) plays aggressively. He curses and is desperate to win. He finally lobs one so fiercely it hurts Joan, the mom (Laura Linney). Frank, the younger son, imitates the Dad by cursing up a storm. Walt, the older son (Jessie Eisenberg), is wary. The family drives home in silence. *(Hint that all is not well—foreshadowing separation.)*

    During dinner, the conversation is uneasy. Walt tries to engage Bernard in a discussion about literature but Bernard pontificates. Frank tries to get attention by shoving nuts up his nose. Not a pleasant meal.

    Walt notices that Bernard has been sleeping on the couch. Bernard makes excuses.

    (More foreshadowing of separation.)

    It's revealed that both parents are writers—Bernard, once published and promising is no longer successful but Joan has recently been published in a literary magazine.

Walt says Bernard is the real writer and tears Joan down. Frank defends her. *(Sons' allegiances are already split.)*

2. Frank is at a tennis lesson with Ivan, the tennis pro (William Baldwin). Bernard challenges Ivan, believing he can win. He ends up exhausted and sweaty.

On the drive home, Bernard tears Ivan down and says the only tennis pro worth being is someone like Andre Agassi or John McEnroe. Frank says he wants to be like Ivan. Bernard makes Frank drive around with him while he finds a parking space. *(Foreshadowing how Frank will behave/react to the separation—whose side he will take.)*

That night, the kids sing a song for their parents. Walt says he wrote it and will play it at a concert at school. Both Joan and Bernard flatter him. *(Parents vie for allegiance of older son.)*

Walt is thrilled with Bernard's comments and asks him to autograph one of the books he wrote.

Bernard writes, "Best Wishes Bernard Berkman (Dad)." Bernard asks Walt to come to the writing class he teaches. *(Foreshadowing how Walt will behave/react to the separation—whose side he will take.)*

In the class, Lili, one of the students (Anna Paquin) reads some sexually graphic poetry. On the ride home with Walt, Bernard praises her and her sexual work and lectures him on literature. On the drive, they see Joan talking to a man on the sidewalk. *(Build up of possibility of reason for the separation.)*

When they get home, Bernard watches his wife writing. The phone rings and he grabs it before she can answer. They fight as the kids listen. *(Confrontation leading up to the separation.)*

3. Bernard announces to the kids that a family conference will be held that night. Joan and Bernard tell the kids that they will separate and explain that they'll have joint custody. Bernard says he has a new house and that they'll split up the week. Walt worries about how he'll get to school and who will get the cat. *(Anxieties caused by separation.)*

Walt accuses Joan of screwing up her marriage of seventeen years. She tells him it has nothing to do with him. *(Older son assigns blame for separation.)*

Later that night, Joan gets books out of the family library and hides them under Frank's bed because she doesn't want Bernard to have them.

On the way to school, Walt tells Frank not to tell anyone. Frank starts crying and says that he has already told everyone. Walt hears from a friend that joint custody "blows." *(Fallout from separation is firmly established.)*

Act Two

4. Bernard drives the kids to his new house and on the way they literally run into Ivan who asks for money. Bernard tells Ivan Joan's paying for the tennis lessons. Bernard calls Ivan a half wit.

    The kids are shocked that Bernard's new house is a dilapidated wreck. Frank is unhappy and says he doesn't like the tennis poster Bernard put up for him and that he misses his pet turtles. Walt tells Frank to be supportive of their dad and says the situation is all mom's doing. Frank calls him a liar and they fight. *(Stress of separation affects Frank and Walt's relationship.)* The next day, Walt is in school and notices a girl named Sophie watching him. He talks to her and parrots his father's view of literature. He sounds pedantic like his dad but the girl seems to like it.

5. Bernard tells Walt that Joan had a four-year affair. Walt is very upset and refuses to stay at Joan's when it's her turn to have the kids. He tells her that it's because she cheated and yells "You disgust me!" He takes his cat and goes to Bernard's. Frank stays.

    Later the boys talk about the affair on the phone. Frank gets graphic as he drinks a beer.

    At school, Frank watches a girl in the library and then goes into the stacks to masturbate.

    Walt tells his friend that his mom and his friend's Dad had an affair and calls his mom an asshole.

    (Sons act out because of separation.)

6. *(First spike in Act Two)* Sophie teaches Walt how to kiss. He tells her she has too many freckles. (His mom has lots of

freckles too!) Bernard's novel is rejected. He lies about it to the kids.

Bernard makes the kids dinner but it falls on the floor. He serves it anyhow and during dinner talks about how he's had lots of opportunities to have affairs but has never done so. He tells them that Joan dropped him because he wasn't successful.

Sophie takes Walt to a Chinese restaurant to meet her family. Bernard brings the cat back to Joan's house. They argue about the cat's food. He says things are going well. She suggests they sit together at Walt's guitar concert and perhaps go out as a family to celebrate his performance. She asks Bernard not to tell the kids about her affairs. He tells her that his father called and suggested there might be a way that he could win Joan back. He tells her that he's tried everything he could think of to make their marriage work and that there was nothing else that he could do. It's clearly over. She says goodbye. *(Divorce imminent.)*

7.   Bernard offers his sexy student a room in his house. She moves in. Walt seems interested in her. Frank and his father play ping pong. The father is obsessed and beats Frank. Frank swears at him.

(Younger son's animosity to Father—not the side he's chosen.)

8.   *(Midpoint)* Walt asks Bernard to go to the movies with him and his date. Bernard suggests they see *Blue Velvet*. They weren't going to see that but Walt acquiesces and he and Sophie are uncomfortable in the theater. In a restaurant after the movie Bernard talks frankly about sex in front of Sophie. She hands him money to pay for the meal and he takes it. Walt looks on, a little uncomfortable. *(Did he choose the wrong side?)*

Frank runs away. Bernard goes looking for him. He's at mom's house where he discovers that his mom is sleeping with Ivan. She also tells Frank that her book is being published.

Bernard picks up Frank who tells him mom is dating Ivan. Bernard calls Ivan un-interesting. Frank defends Ivan. Bernard asks Frank to have dinner with him. Frank refuses.

Walt makes out with Sophie and admits he's a virgin. *(Youngest kid discovers his mom has a lover who he likes. This reveals how emotionally complicated the social issue can become.)*

9.   Lili tells Bernard that she'll show his book to an agent. Lili flatters Bernard and kisses him. He asks her to go out of town to one of his readings. Walt tells Sophie they should wait to have sex.

Frank spreads semen on a locker at school. *(More acting out!)*

Walt wins the school talent show for the song he's written. Bernard is there with Lili, mom is there with Ivan. Everyone compliments Walt. Mom asks him out to dinner to celebrate and he walks out on her, giving her the finger. *(Emotional trauma increases.)*

On the way out, someone compliments her on the excerpt of her novel in the *New Yorker*. Bernard looks on, cringing.

He tells Walt to sleep with Sophie but see other women.

10.   Walt breaks up with Sophie. *(Father has huge influence on the older boy continuing to pay off earlier foreshadowing but he's conflicted.)*

He goes home and sees Lili who tells him she knows he plagiarized his winning song from Pink Floyd *(Evidence of older boy acting out.)*

Walt leans forward to kiss her leg and they knock heads. Lili gets a bloody nose. The moment is over. Walt leaves but then sees Bernard knocking on Lili's door.

Frank is at his mom's and wants to stay there but she and Ivan are going out of town.

Frank calls his dad. There's no answer. He pours himself some booze.

Meanwhile, Bernard, Walt and Lili are driving to the reading.

11.   *(Second spike in Act Two)* Frank is home alone. He tries on a condom, drinks and throws up. Joan and Bernard sit in the principal's office listening to her talk about Frank. She tells them he's been masturbating in the library and that he smeared semen on a locker. She asks them if anything has happened at home recently that would make him act this way. Joan says that Bernard left him home alone for an entire weekend. Bernard

blames it on Joan for divorcing him. Joan says Bernard is living with a twenty-year-old. Bernard tells Joan to stay out of his life. *(Separation and its results out in the open.)*

The school knows Walt stole lyrics from Pink Floyd and he will have to return the prize money. Also, Walt isn't doing his schoolwork. The principal suggests that Bernard talk to Walt and that Walt needs to see a therapist.

At the therapist, Walt rationalizes his song theft by saying that he could have written the song and so he said he did. He looks at it as a technicality. *(Divorce trauma has affected clear thinking.)*

The therapist asks him for a nice memory. Walt talks about watching Robin Hood with his mother and how much he appreciated her telling him the story of a battle between a squid and a whale based on an exhibit at the Natural History Museum. He makes no mention of Bernard. *(Older son's loyalties are becoming even more confused.)*

12. Bernard is forcing himself on Lili as Walt walks in. Walt runs off. *(Older son realizes his loyalty to his father might be misplaced.)* Bernard looks for Walt everywhere and finally goes to Joan's house. He asks Frank to come over. Frank doesn't want to. *(Younger son is sure of his loyalty.)*

Walt goes to the Chinese restaurant where he knows Sophie and her family will be eating. He watches them through the window.

He goes to the park, sticks his head in the lake and then goes back to Joan's house where he finds Frank drinking beer.

Walt realizes he shouldn't have broken up with Sophie but says he did because he thought he could do better. *(Acting on his father's bad advice.)*

13. Joan tells Walt that she did love Bernard.

Bernard shows up and asks to save the marriage. He says he made every effort and he wants to talk more about it. *(Father realizes he has lost the affection of both his sons and tries to change things.)* Joan breaks out laughing. Bernard gets angry and tells Joan he'll sue her for full custody. She says he only wanted joint custody because it was cheaper. *(Divorce justified.)*

The cat escapes and Bernard goes after him. Because he's double parked he gets a ticket and freaks out. He collapses on the pavement.

Act Three

14. Bernard reminds Joan of things in their past. He's taken away by ambulance with Walt and Ivan. Frank and Joan look for the cat. *(Younger son and mother are united.)*

15. Walt arrives at the hospital and Bernard asks him to stay for the day. He says that Lili has moved out.
    Walt asks to stay at Joan's more. Says he doesn't want to be at Bernard's for awhile. *(Walt tries to break away and become his own person. He's further alienated by the divorce.)*
    Bernard tells him that hurts his feelings and says that if Walt stays with him he'll redo his room and offers him a copy of a rare book. Walt cries. Bernard takes his hand. He asks Walt to get him a pillow. Walt leaves the hospital as if he's escaping.
    He goes to the squid and whale exhibit at the Natural History Museum. *(A metaphor for the social issue—two powerful people in their struggle give kids the impossible task of choosing allegiances.)*

You'll notice how, because this is a really short film, the act breaks and spikes are not in their usual positions. You'll also notice how the plot points still reinforce the important story point just as they should and emphasize the social issue.

The Squid and the Whale is a *Heart-Tugger* because it focuses on the relationships of four people and their inter-connectedness. This inter-connectedness makes up the entire fabric of the movie whose purpose is to show the effect of separation and divorce on the relationship between parents and children. It's very successful in doing that. Other films using this model may emphasize the relationship between two people (as in *Dead Man Walking*) or even more (in some war issue films companies or platoons are featured) as they play out the social issue but in all cases, in this model, relationships are what drives the social issue, gives it meaning, depth and context. The key to this model is the revelation of characters and their interaction as a result of the social issue.

Here are some other examples of *The Heart-Tugger:*

The Visitor (2007): A professor becomes involved with illegal immigrants and it changes his life (immigration issues).

Juno (2007): A quirky pregnant teenager forms a relationship with the couple she chooses to adopt her baby (abortion, teen pregnancy).

Dead Man Walking (1995): The relationship between a nun and a convicted killer (capital punishment).

Leaving Las Vegas (1995): The relationship between an alcoholic determined to drink himself to death and the prostitute who promises not to interfere with his plans (alcoholism).

War of the Roses (1989): A couple's vicious divorce battle. Even though it's a comedy it fits into the Heart-Tugger category.

Casablanca (1942): An expatriate sacrifices an ardent love for something more noble in time of war (war issues).

Exercise

Name and outline another *Heart-Tugger*.

The Yoda: The Mentor Model

This model can be tricky because there are lots of *Heart-Tugger* elements to it. The mentor is indeed in a relationship with one or more of the other main characters but the thing that makes the model *Yoda*, is that besides having a relationship with the character, the mentor is in a position of authority, talking from a place of expertise and employs instruction and/or counsel to get the character through the dilemma posed by the social issue.

In *The Yoda*, the film can start with focus on the mentor or it can start with the focus on the character involved in the social issue as he or she searches for a mentor or comes upon one. The mentor doesn't even have to appear in the first act. Much like what we've seen in the *Sherlock/Snitch* where the whistleblower can be identified later in the film, the mentor can come upon the scene at a crucial structure point in a dramatic way when the problem reaches its zenith. Keep in mind that the mentor in this model doesn't always have to be a teacher or a shrink. It's often the case but *The Yoda* can have as its' core a good friend or a parent—virtually any one in a position to guide and help.

The King's Speech (2010)

Written by: David Seidler
Directed by Tom Hooper
Starring: Colin Firth, Geoffrey Rush, Helena Bonham Carter
Social issue: Disabilities.

The King's Speech is the true story of England's King George VI who suffered from a life-long stutter, and the speech therapist who helped him overcome it enough to make crucial speeches.

This film is interesting because it shows how a relationship is crucial to *The Yoda*. At the same time it demonstrates how this relationship can take a back seat to the importance of actual professional instruction and/or social dictates. Lionel Logue, the therapist (Geoffrey Rush) struggles to stand on common ground with Bertie, the Duke of York (Colin Firth) and with Bertie the King and is sometimes allowed to do so only because of his ability and insight as a mentor.

Act One

1. Establishes the importance of speeches in the royal role and demonstrates the agony experienced by Bertie when he's forced to give a speech. *(Disability and its discomfort introduced and demonstrated.)*
2. Introduction of the speech therapy process and a "bad" therapist. Bertie reacts badly.
    He tells his wife Elizabeth (Helena Bonham Carter) that he will suffer no more teachers.
    Elizabeth goes to Harley Street and finds a set of dilapidated rooms.
    She meets Lionel Logue (Geoffrey Rush) who doesn't know who she is but says that he can cure her husband if he wants to be cured *(Page Ten Hook—Introduction of the yoda.)*
3. Logue insists that her husband come by and play by his rules.
    Elizabeth confesses that her husband is the Duke of York.
    Elizabeth emphasizes the need for total discretion.

Logue emphasizes his need for trust and total equality in his consulting rooms.

Even though she thinks his methods are unorthodox, Elizabeth asks him to start. *(Inciting incident—the yoda's help requested.)*

Logue goes home to his family and tells them he has a new patient but doesn't say who it is. *(Yoda's discretion demonstrated.)*

Bertie and Elizabeth are with their family. Their girls want Bertie to tell them a story. He's reluctant but agrees, making every effort to overcome his stammer. *(Need for help with discomfort disability causes even in private is demonstrated.)*

4. The first mention of Wallis Simpson and her relationship with Bertie's brother and heir to the throne, the Prince of Wales.

   Logue goes to an audition and is complimented on his diction although he doesn't get the part.

   (Professional recognition of the yoda's abilities with speech provides a contrast to what we've already seen of Bertie's ability.)

   Bertie and Elizabeth go to Logue's place and are confronted by a little child who speaks haltingly but well. *(Example of the yoda's handiwork.)*

   Bertie meets Logue. *(Reinforcement of inciting incident.)*

5. Bertie is shocked at Logue's familiarity and attempts at friendly chatter. He is reluctant to use first names with Logue or to answer any personal questions. He wants to leave.

   Logue cajoles him into staying longer by making a bet that if Bertie can read without stammering he will pay Logue a shilling and agree to his terms. *(The yoda's method of working with clients demonstrated.)*

6. Logue hands Bertie a book but Bertie is reluctant to read it and refuses. Logue reminds him of their bet and as a gentleman, Bertie must keep his word. He takes the book as Logue plays loud music as he records Bertie's reading.

   Half-way through the reading, Bertie gives up and tells Logue that the treatments are not for him.

   Logue gives Bertie the recording of the reading to play later. *(The yoda's persistence demonstrated.)*

At the palace, Bertie's father, the King (Michael Gambon) tells him he'll have to give a speech and talks about the relationship between Wallis and the Prince of Wales. Bertie's father browbeats him. *(Stigma and pain of disability emphasized.)*

Devastated and depressed, and in a state of self loathing, Bertie listens to the phonograph record.

He hears himself reading without stammering. *(The yoda's methods can work. The disabled person is given hope that the disability can be conquered.) (End Act One.)*

Act Two

7. Elizabeth and Bertie go back to Logue's shabby consulting rooms.

    Bertie wants to continue on a strictly business basis with no personal stuff mixed in.

    He asks if Logue is willing to work on mechanics and to assist him in events. Logue agrees but says he'll have to see Bertie daily. *(The yoda will do anything necessary to engage the person who needs his help.)*

8. Logue goes through various bizarre physical exercises with Bertie.

    Logue won't let Bertie smoke. *(The yoda's unorthodox methods demonstrated and the disabled person's willingness to do what it takes to cure his problem.)*

9. *(First spike in Second Act)*

    David, the Prince of Wales (Guy Pearce), is introduced and the severity of the situation with Wallis is demonstrated.

    The King dies.

    Everyone (including Bertie) bows to David who breaks down. *(The person suffering from the disability believes he might be "saved" from demonstrating it publically but he's on shaky ground.)*

10. Bertie goes to see Lionel and says he has been practicing an hour a day.

    He asks for a drink and begins to talk personally. *(The yoda has won some trust.)*

    Logue continues with the session and when Bertie has trouble expressing himself about personal matters, Logue tells him to sing the words. Bertie refuses. *(The yoda isn't completely trusted. Client is unwilling to look or feel foolish in his presence.)*

11. Logue bribes Bertie into talking about his feelings about David.

    Bertie tells Logue it's a relief he knows he won't be king.

    Bertie reveals much more about his early life and his relationship with his father and with David.

    He exposes the ways in which he was abused as a child.

    Bertie is abashed at his "confessions." Lionel tells him that they are friends. *(Significant gain in trust by the yoda.)*

12. *(Midpoint)* Elizabeth and Bertie go to David's party where they meet Wallis Simpson for the first time. Elizabeth is rude to her and Winston Churchill agrees with Elizabeth's treatment of her. David tells Bertie he intends to marry Wallis. Bertie knows that means David can't remain king. *(Disability sufferer realized that his hopes of "hiding" his disability from the public may be futile.)*

13. Bertie tells David he's trying to cure his stammer. David makes fun of him and accuses Bertie of trying to push him off the throne. Bertie can't reply because he's caught in a terrible moment of stammering. *(Stigma, discomfort and pain of disability again emphasized.)*

    Bertie goes to see Logue and tells him he froze.

    Logue encourages Bertie and finds out that Bertie doesn't stammer when he swears.

    They go walking and Bertie tells Logue about Wallis and that he'll do anything in his power to keep David on the throne. Logue tells Bertie he could be king. Bertie becomes furious and accuses Logue of treason. He insults Logue and tells him their sessions are over. *(The yoda goes farther than his client is willing to go.)*

14. Official objections to Wallis are posed and discussed.

    Lionel is upset over the situation with Bertie and still doesn't tell his wife who he is. He realizes he over-stepped and goes to the Palace to apologize.

    Bertie refuses to see him. *(The yoda is willing to admit his mistake and is willing to do what it takes to get client to return.*

Disability sufferer hangs on to the chance he can still hide from the public.)

Churchill tells Bertie that parliament won't support the marriage of David and Wallis.

Bertie tells Churchill that David is not of sound mind at the moment.

Churchill suggests that Bertie choose a name for himself as king.

(The disability sufferer realizes he can no longer hide his disability. He is afraid and miserable.)

15. *(Second spike in Act Two)*

    David abdicates.

    Bertie succeeds him. He addresses a room full of people and has trouble speaking. *(Disability emphasized again.)*

    He is horrified at having to do the Christmas broadcast and breaks down. *(Anxiety about disability reaches new heights. Need for the yoda is emphasized.)*

16. Bertie and Elizabeth goes to see Logue at Logue's home and Bertie apologizes as much as he's able to.

    Logue asks him in and while Elizabeth takes tea (Logue's wife is out) Logue counsels Bertie and encourages him. *(The yoda expertly picks up where they left off with no resentment.)*

    Logue's wife arrives home and he introduces her to the royals. They are a surprise. She has never known Logue was treating Bertie. *(The maintenance of the yoda's discretion and integrity in spite of set-backs is emphasized.)*

17. Preparations for Bertie's coronation in Westminster Abbey are under way.

    Bertie introduces Logue and tells the Archbishop of Canterbury that Logue will be sitting in the royal box. The Archbishop is miffed and shocked that Logue is not someone chosen as a royal physician but agrees to the king's request to let Logue stay. *(The yoda is championed by his acolyte.)*

18. *(End of Act Two)* Bertie confronts Logue and says he's discovered that Logue has no diploma or qualifications. *(The yoda's acolyte gets cold feet and isn't sure about him.)*

Logue talks about his work with war veterans but admits he's not a doctor. *(The yoda is honest but resolute that he can help his acolyte.)*

Bertie accuses Logue of wanting to snare a celebrity patient and not really wanting to help. *(The acolyte questions the motivations of the yoda.)*

Logue stands tough and confronts Bertie. They argue. *(The yoda refuses to back down.)*

Logue compliments Bertie's perseverance and reassures him that he has a voice. *(The yoda insists his motivations are pure.)*

The Archbishop tells Logue he's through.

Bertie reconsiders and says he'll keep working with Logue. *(The acolyte finally and ultimately accepts the yoda unconditionally.)*

Act Three

19.   Logue helps Bertie rehearse for the coronation.

    Bertie watches the film of the coronation and everyone is pleased at how well he did.

    Then Bertie watches a newsreel of Hitler and is uncomfortable at how well Hitler speaks. *(The disability is still troubling when the sufferer compares himself to others more capable.)*

    Churchill gives a powerful speech declaring war with Germany. *(Another contrast with the sufferer.)*

20.   Bertie must give a speech to the nation in a live broadcast. He asks for Logue. *(At his most trying moment, acolyte puts faith in the yoda.)*

    Logue puts Bertie through his paces as he practices the speech. *(The yoda is up for the task.)*

    Bertie feels powerless because he can't speak for the nation. He swears and sings bits of the speech to try and get it right. Churchill confesses that he once had a speech impediment and encourages Bertie. *(In the face of the disability, people are sympathetic and encouraging.)*

21.   Logue tells Bertie to deliver the speech as if he were speaking to a friend. He prepares Bertie.

    Bertie thanks Logue. *(The acolyte is grateful to the yoda for his help and support.)*

Bertie gives the speech as Logue coaches him through it. *(The yoda is there for the acolyte in his moment of need.)*

22. The speech is a success.

Logue compliments Bertie. *(The yoda is proud of his acolyte and acknowledges his accomplishment.)*

Everyone congratulates Bertie. *(The acolyte has accomplished much.)*

Logue looks on, smiling proudly. *(The yoda has achieved his purpose.)*

Significantly, the last shot in the film is of Logue. Because the movie ends on him, it reinforces the importance of the yoda and emphasizes the achievement of the master rather than his acolyte. This film then, obviously demonstrates how important the mentor can be to the resolution or amelioration of a problem created by a social issue.

More examples of *The Yoda*:

Educating Rita (1983): With the help of a professor, an uneducated British working class girl excels in school and gains the confidence she needs to improve her life (education).

Good Will Hunting (1997): A psychologist helps a gifted school janitor find direction (education).

The Soloist (2009): A true story of a journalist who tries to make life better for a homeless Juilliard trained musician (homelessness, mental health).

Exercise

Come up with another example of *The Yoda* and outline it.

The Shining Knight: The Hero Rescuer Model

The key to this model is positioning the hero/rescuer as the main character. That figure must be a person of conscience and ability although he/she may not be conscious of that ability at the beginning of the film. Lots of heroes are in fact ordinary people who do extraordinary things by digging deep inside themselves to discover their hidden inner resources and strengths. These resources and strengths are then used effectively to solve or ameliorate the problem posed by the social issue involved.

The social issue may be huge but the shining knight in this model takes it on, often at great personal cost, and does what he/she can to contribute to its solution even in a small way. And that small way sometimes turns out to be very huge indeed.

Hotel Rwanda (2004)

Written by: Kier Pearson and Terry George
Directed by: Terry George
Starring: Don Cheadle and Sophie Okonedo
Social issue: Genocide.

Hotel Rwanda is a prime example of *The Shining Knight*. It tells the true story of Paul Rusesabagina, the manager of a four-star Rwandan hotel who saved over 1,200 lives by harboring refugees there. Paul (played by Don Cheadle who got an Academy Award nomination for his performance) is a soft-spoken, efficient man who takes pride in running a first class establishment for his Belgian bosses. He cultivates many friends among the military by plying them with top-shelf single-malt whiskey and Cuban cigars hoping they'll be there for him if he needs them.

When the Hutus begin systematically slaughtering Tutsis in the genocide of 1994 he is appalled. He is a Hutu and his wife is a Tutsi and besides fearing for his own family's life, he sees the killing as senseless, stupid and immoral. That's when he calls in his favors to great effect and manages to become a hero.

Because the social issue is a political one and comes out of the fabric of the African atmosphere at the time, the audience is caught up in the action even before the film begins in an over-black voice-over that talks about the Hutu-Tutsi conflict.

Act One

1. Kigali 1994. The audience is introduced to the Kigali atmosphere as Paul (the Knight) drives through it to the airport where he picks up boxes of Cuban cigars—obviously contraband.

    He explains to his driver Dube that these cigars are necessary in business to show style while persuading people. *(Foreshadowing his future actions with regard to genocide.)*

As his hotel's food distributor lights up one of the cigars, the man invites Paul to a Hutu rally and urges him to join Hutu ranks to fight against Tutsis.

Paul sees a crate dropped in the warehouse. It's full of machetes. *(Foreshadowing of genocide.)*

On the way back, he hears talk telling Hutus to kill Tutsis and doesn't believe it will happen because it will hurt business. *(Possibility of genocide is introduced here and knight's reaction to it.)*

2. Paul and Dube drive through the Hutu rally on their way home. Dube is worried because he is a Tutsi and the Hutus at the rally are out for blood. Paul protects Dube by holding up a Hutu shirt.

   (Foreshadowing again and revealing knight's protective character and non-discrimination against Tutsis.)

   Back at the hotel, Paul demonstrates his ingenuity and managerial skills.

   The United Nations Colonel Oliver (Nick Nolte) is worried about the problem but Paul's friend General Bizimungu (Fana Mokolna), who he's plied with the best single malt scotch, promises to control the Hutus.

   As Paul drives home, the radio warns about Tutsi rebels and he changes the station to hear that the U.N. is trying to broker a peace agreement. The streets are filling up with soldiers.

   (Political machinations of situation revealed.)

3. A dinner at home with his extended family is interrupted by a police action outside. Paul and his wife see his neighbors being beaten and taken away by soldiers. *(Inciting incident.)*

   Even so, Paul does nothing because he doesn't want to endanger his family. *(Knight's protective nature emphasized but at this point it's exclusive to his family.)*

   He tells his brother-in-law and his family to stay overnight and explains that the neighbor was denounced as a rebel spy by someone. When Paul's wife Tatania asks him to call one of his contacts to intervene, he says that his contacts are to help his family in case something should happen and the neighbors are not family. He refuses to call but he's troubled.

Exposition about the difference between Hutus and Tutsis—
an artificial division created by Belgians. *(Root of conflict
causing genocide explained.)*

4. Paul is told by his friend the warehouse manager that he and
his family must leave.

    He reveals that things are getting worse and at the signal "cut
the tall trees" killing will begin.

    Paul counters, saying that the U.N. is there and a peace accord
was signed.

    When his brother-in-law and sister-in-law tell him they want
to leave because they are afraid of the coming violence, he
urges them to trust in the peace process and to go home and
stop worrying.

    On his way home he sees fires and fighting in the streets and
hears a police order for people to stay in their houses.

    He comes home to a dark house and finds his wife, kids
and Tutsi neighbors taking refuge in a back room. His
neighbors are there because they trust him. And his wife is
Tutsi.

    They tell him the President who signed the peace accord is
dead and the phone lines have been cut. He tells them to
remain calm. *(Genocide threat accelerates.)*

5. His young son is missing. He's discovered in the neighbor's
yard covered in blood. He's hysterical but not hurt. The blood
isn't his. It's obvious that the neighbors have been murdered.

    A news broadcast blames the President's death on the Tutsis
and calls for the Hutus to arm themselves.

    Soldiers arrive at the house and demand keys to the Diplomat
hotel where Paul used to work. Paul convinces them to take
everyone in the house to his hotel after he's given the soldiers
the keys they want. As they drive, he and his family sees the
neighbors dead on the lawn. *(Genocide demonstrated.)*

6. *(End Act One)* People are dragged from their homes, shot and
killed. Paul arrives at the Diplomat hotel, opens the safe and
pockets some U.S. money.

    He gives the commanding soldier the keys but the soldier
orders everyone out of the van and tells Paul he must shoot

them because they are Tutsis. If he does that, his own family will be saved. The commander puts a gun to Paul's head but he refuses and instead offers the man money. He gives him the American money he took from the safe. The commander wants more.

Paul tells him he'll give him more money if they go to his hotel. The soldiers can keep the neighbors and his family outside until he gets the money. The commander agrees. *(Knight's negotiating abilities demonstrated in a move away from "only my family" stance.)*

He gives the money to the commander who orders his soldiers to leave. His neighbors and family flee into the hotel and to safety. *(Genocide tension heightened.)*

Act Two

7. Paul tries to control staff at his hotel.

   He puts his neighbors in staff rooms.

   The Americans at the hotel are trying to get answers. He calms them down.

   Gregoire, one of his Hutu employees, moves into the presidential suite and refuses to work, threatening to expose the Tutsis who are hiding at the hotel.

   More Tutsis arrive and are told to share rooms.

   Children from an orphanage are brought to the hotel by the Red Cross. He takes them in. *(Knight's benevolence kicks in.)*

8. He agrees to take another ten children if the Red Cross worker will try and locate his brother-in-law and his family. *(Knight's negotiating skills again demonstrated.)*

   He tells his wife he's worried about lowering the tone of the hotel and losing his job.

   He checks on the orphans and asks one of his staff to take care of them. *(Knight's benevolence emphasized in spite of his reservations.)*

   The U.N. Colonel explains the U.N. is not allowed to intervene. He refuses to help, saying his forces are overwhelmed. He promises everything will be taken care of when the situation stabilizes.

A camera man wants to cover trouble in the countryside. His boss refuses to let him.

Paul tells the staff he's now their boss. He calls the Belgian hotel owner who wonders if the hotel should be closed.

Paul says that the hotel is an oasis of calm and that the U.N. has everything under control.

(Knight's desperation to help people overcomes his reluctance to stick his neck out.)

9. *(First spike in Second Act)* Paul asks the owner to send a letter from Belgium telling the staff to perform its duties.

    He tears it up and tells the staff anyone can leave who wants to. They all stay. *(Knight establishes himself in control.)*

    Paul goes to the journalist's room to fix an air conditioner. While he's there, the camera man comes back with explosive footage of the killing fields.

    Paul watches the footage of a massacre in horror. Hutus are killing Tutsis and there are women and children among the victims. *(Knight gets even more visual proof to reinforce his purpose and motivation.)*

    He tells the camera man that he's seen the footage and that he hopes people will intervene when they see such atrocities. The camera man doesn't believe anyone will do anything.

    Refugees desperate for safety storm the gates of the hotel. The U.N. follows.

    U.N. says that the Hutus have surrounded the hotel.

    Hutus arrive and have showdown with U.N. The Hutus back down and leave.

    (Genocide is at the door.)

10. The Red Cross worker tells Paul that his brother-in-law's house is empty but that his two little girls are safe with a neighbor. He asks her to go back for the girls. She says she can't because all the roads are blocked.

    She tells him they killed the children at the orphanage and made her watch. *(Genocide reinforced.)*

Paul tells her he believes an intervention force will arrive soon to restore order. The French arrive and everyone rejoices, thinking the trouble is over.

Colonel Oliver reveals that the West doesn't care about Africans and that the intervention forces are not going to stay or stop the killings. *(Knight realizes he's in this all alone.)*

11. Paul tells his wife the news. *(Knight acknowledges the horrible truth.)*

    All the whites are being evacuated from the hotel.

    The U.N. can only spare four men to guard the hotel.

    The whites and journalists leave the hotel.

    The U.N. refuses to take the orphans to safety.

12. *(Midpoint)* Paul takes the orphans into the hotel.

    Paul's wife tells him she wants him to take the kids and go to safety. He refuses.

    (Knight's willingness to sacrifice himself for others.)

    Paul wakes up with a gun to his head. He is told that everyone must leave the hotel at once.

    He negotiates a ten-minute reprieve while he calls everyone he knows. Finally, he calls his Belgian boss and tells him that the Hutu army has ordered everyone out of the hotel and if 800 "guests" and 100 staff don't leave, they'll all be killed. *(Danger of the situation emphasized. Knights ingenuity and failure to give in demonstrated.)*

13. Paul tells his boss it's the French who are supplying the Hutus. His boss tells Paul he'll try and help but Paul has to stall for time. Paul manages to stall the soldiers and just as they are about to kill everyone, the soldiers are ordered to leave. *(Knight's ingenuity and resourcefulness win the day.)*

    The Belgian boss tells Paul he called the French Prime Minister to get the soldiers to stand down.

    He tells Paul there will be no rescue and that they must all save themselves. *(Knight once again confronted by the grim reality and sees he can't rely on anyone for help.)*

    He tells the refugees that they must save themselves by calling all the influential people they know abroad and shame them into sending help. *(Knight gets tough and real.)*

14.   Paul determines that he has to convince people in power that it's still a four-star hotel so he presents the refugees with bills. America refuses to call the Rwandan situation genocide.

General Bizimungu tells Paul he'll take care of him since his white friends have abandoned him.

Paul tells the general he will be rewarded but also that the Americans and the U.N. will watch everything with satellites. He's impressed and worried.

Paul gets him to intimidate Gregoire into going back to work. *(Knight demonstrates smarts in getting help.)*

Paul tells Tatiana that he has to leave the hotel to get food. He says he'll take Gregoire with him.

15.   *(Second spike in Act Two)* Paul and Gregoire leave the hotel and go to food warehouse.

Radio announcer tells Hutus to rape Tutsi women. Paul sees women being brutalized. *(Genocide fallout demonstrated again.)*

Paul pays double price for goods and is refused whiskey.

The warehouse manager believes all the Tutsis can be killed. *(Genocide emphasized.)*

The warehouse manager says the Hutus will eventually get rid of the general protecting the hotel.

He urges Paul to give up all the Tutsis at the hotel and his family will be saved. Paul refuses.

He tells Paul to take the River Road back home.

Paul and Gregoire find the road hard going. It's foggy. Paul gets out and sees that the road is lined with bodies. *(Genocide emphasized visually.)*

16.   It's a sight Paul has never seen. He tells Gregoire to back up. They have to run over bodies to do that. He tells Gregoire to tell no one what they've seen.

Paul comes home and breaks down. *(Knight's vulnerability and horror in the face of genocide demonstrated.)*

17.   In a romantic moment Paul takes Tatiana up to the roof for drinks. He tells her they must have a plan. If he is killed he makes her promise to take the children and jump off the roof. She resists but finally promises. *(Knight is practical and tough in the face of horror.)*

The U. N. arrives with exit visas for some families.

Paul and his family get visas for Belgium.

18. *(End of Act Two)* Tatiana says she wants to find her brother's children and take them too.

    Paul asks the Red Cross worker to look for the kids. She tells him they are probably dead.

    He promises to find a country to take the orphans and she agrees to go looking for the kids.

    The refugees say goodbye to Paul and thank him.

    Everyone who has exit visas gets on the U.N. truck.

    He tells Tatiana they can't wait for the girls any longer. She gets on the truck with the kids.

    At the last moment, Paul refuses to go. *(Knight makes huge sacrifice to finish his job.)*

Act Three

19. Radio announcement threatens Hutus who shelter Tutsis as the U.N. truck travels to the airport.

    The radio orders Hutus to stop the trucks.

    Paul is told that Gregoire told the Hutu military that the refugees were going.

    Paul knows the truck is driving into an ambush.

    The truck is stopped and Colonel Oliver refuses to let the armed Hutus search it.

    They go into the truck anyhow and start hurting people with machetes.

    The army arrives just in time to stop a Hutu from killing Tatiana.

    The Hutus leave and the truck drives back to the hotel.

    When they arrive Tatiana is furious at Paul for leaving her.

20. The water in the hotel is shut off. *(Situation is grave re health concerns.)*

    General Bizimungu confronts Paul and asks him for more bribes. He refuses Rwandan money which he says is useless.

    He drives off saying he'll give Paul no more protection because he's out of whiskey.

    A rocket is fired into the hotel.

Colonel Oliver tells Paul that the Hutus have agreed to a prisoner exchange—the refugees for Hutus—and they can do it in two days. Paul says they'll all be dead in two days.

Thinking about it in a quiet moment, he remembers the safe at the Diplomat hotel.

On his way there, he sees the ruined Red Cross truck and assumes that the woman he sent to find his brother-in-law's kids is dead. He sees troops shooting at unarmed civilians. *(Genocide again emphasized. Knight is determined to act even in face of the hopeless situation.)*

21.   At the Diplomat hotel, Paul opens the safe and gives the general jewelry and booze.

The general tells Paul he'll take him to Hutu headquarters where he'll be safe.

Paul says he must go back to the hotel for his family. The general refuses to let him.

Paul tells the general that he's at the top of a list of war criminals and will be persecuted for genocide. He offers to tell the Americans that the general is innocent if he'll let him go back to the hotel. The general refuses. Paul says he's willing to die but then no one will testify on the general's behalf.

The general backs down. The general reluctantly agrees. *(Knight is cool in the face of obstacle.)*

When Paul gets back to the hotel, it's in chaos. Soldiers are everywhere and people are being rounded up.

Panicked, he rushes to the roof thinking that his wife and children may have jumped.

22.   Paul's family is not on the roof. He finds them huddled in a bathtub.

The U.N. loads Paul and his family onto trucks and locks the hotel.

They travel toward Tutsi rebel lines to get to safety.

On the way they see Hutus burning villages and shooting. They see thousands of Hutu refugees fleeing.

Hutu soldiers are gunned down by Tutsi rebels as the trucks make it to safety behind the front lines.

23.　They arrive at a refugee camp.

Paul and his family are ordered to get on a bus to Tanzania.

Tatiana asks about her brother's girls but there's no time to find them.

They board the bus.

The Red Cross worker, who was not killed after all, recognizes one of the orphans from the hotel. She rushes to the bus and pulls Paul and his family off. She re-unites them with the lost kids. They all board the bus to safety.

Because this story was based on a real person, it's even more compelling. Each one of Paul's acts of bravery is significant and poignant. The real Paul Rusesabagina was a true shining knight who ended up saving the lives of many people. His actions described systematically at critical screenplay structure points in this model, made this particular social issue (genocide) frighteningly real to audiences everywhere.

More examples of *The Shining Knight*:

The Blind Side (2009): A caring woman and her family take in a homeless teen and help him become an all-American football player (education, poverty).

A Civil Action (1998): An attorney sacrifices everything to expose toxic waste dumping (public health, corporate greed).

Schindler's List (1993): Oskar Schindler saves Jews during the Holocaust (genocide).

Exercise

Come up with another example of *The Shining Knight* and outline it.

As you do these exercises, keep in mind that models can be blended. For example, *The Blind Side* is a *Shining Knight* with *The Yoda* and *The Heart-Tugger* thrown in. The Tuohy family (particularly the mom Leigh Ann (Sandra Bullock) rescues Michael. He's mentored by S.J. and the family and it demonstrates relationship intricacies. However, ultimately *The Blind Side* fits *The Shining Knight* model because of the heroic "rescue" tactics of Leigh Ann which over-shadow the other elements.

When you're studying the model examples and other films that match them, you should notice what other model elements appear in each so you can understand how models may be blended to make sure that audiences are given lots of ways to relate to the social issue at hand.

8

RESEARCH

Once you've chosen your issue, determined who your characters are and how you want to attack your story, you'll need to make sure that you've got your facts right and all the information you need to write your screenplay. That's where research comes in. But wait! While research can help you flush out or even come up with a story (as we'll see later), it can also mess you up big time.

Basic Ground Rules

When it comes to writing about social issues, lots of screenwriters fall into information quicksand. They're convinced they've got to know every little detail about their issue before they start writing. That's just plain wrong. In fact, lots of writers use research as an excuse to keep from writing. Those writers will tell you that they can't really tell their story until their brains are chocked full of facts, statistics, implications and nuances. They spend weeks, months, even years, pounding beats in libraries and trolling the web instead of writing. This "brilliant" stall technique leaves writers overwhelmed, confused and terrified. They end up with mountains of scrawled notes, but no script.

Because the issue resonates with you, you probably already know lots about it—certainly enough to make a start. To paraphrase Bob Dylan, if you're standing in a hurricane you don't need a meteorologist to tell you it's windy. The main thing you need to discover is how to find your way into the issue by creating a compelling story. At this point you've got three options.

The first involves creating a screenplay about a real person involved in the issue you've chosen. We tend to think we become aware of an issue through osmosis but that isn't true. Most often, we become aware through our experiences with real people whose pain, frustration or joy we can feel and relate to. If you can find a real person who's had a specific social issue affect his/her life, you can use him/her to tell the story of your movie.

You can find out lots of information about that issue through simply following that person as he/she negotiates his/her way through, into and around it. If your story focuses on that person and is entirely about his/her experience, you may need to get the rights to that person's story (you've got some other options here and we've explored them in the "True or False" section) and then tell it from his/her point of view. That's pretty much a no-brainer. It's easy to get the primary essential details of an issue from a real person and easier still to define the story. You can check them out or you can decide to write your movie as an "as told to" which means that you're basing it all on the real person's version of events and even diaries, documents, and letters that person will share with you.

Next, you could write your movie based on a real incident/event that comes out of the issue you're showcasing. If you're adapting a story from an existing non-fiction book or article, you've got to decide what facts and information you want to use to make your movie effective and arrange that information to conform to proper screenplay structure.

Lots of books have been written that will tell you how to adapt a book into a movie and it is too complicated a process to go into in-depth here. Briefly though, you'll want to select those incidents in the book that are the most visual and congruent and that connect to make a complete story. You've got to decide which tangents and details are unnecessary and you've got to select characters to help you get the audience into your subject.

Fortunately, all the research you need will be right there in the book. For example, when William Goldman wrote *All the President's Men* (based on the book of the same name by Carl Bernstein and Bob Woodward), he used the actual authors as characters to tell the story through. He used pivotal information in that book to build his screenplay by revealing important facts at crucial structure points in the film. It was a great example of the Investigation/Whistleblower model.

Most of the time though (the third option), you'll want to jump off the cliff and come up with everything—characters, incidents, events— from scratch. To do that, you'll need to create your own characters by conjuring up an amalgam of the characters you've known (see the list you made in a previous chapter) and ones you've imagined. Your characters will need to have sensitivities to particular issues because of things that have happened to them in their pasts. You'll also need to find a point at which the underlying issue comes to a head—a point at which the issue moves to the forefront of your characters' lives. That point will most probably serve as the inciting incident in your screenplay so it needs to be significant and effective.

That's where research comes in. Usually these "come-to-a-head" situations are prompted by significant facts and events that are well documented. Let's take a hypothetical example. If you are writing about the issue of poverty for instance, your characters can be poor and can have led poor and miserable lives with lots of deprivation and want in the past but have somehow gotten by until one of them needs life-saving medical treatment that is entirely unaffordable. You've just heard on the news that a new medical treatment is available to cure a certain disease but it is prohibitively expensive.

You may believe that this treatment should be made available at a much lower cost. This could motivate you to research the ways in which indigent people can receive medical care and what you discover would give you the steps your characters take to get the new treatment and ultimately, give you the story you are looking for.

You may discover in your research that this new care is ultimately unattainable and you can then, through evolving the tension caused by that, show how your characters overcome that obstacle or succumb to it. In your research you may even find examples of people who have done both. Inspired by the examples discovered in your research, you can make a definitive statement about poverty and about medical care. Two issues in one! Having a point of reference (event) to pin the research on (in this case a new medical treatment), will make that research easier and less overwhelming.

What's more difficult is finding your way into an issue you care deeply about through a story you create out of whole cloth with no real and topical "inciting incident" or published material. The way to do that is to involve yourself with research that will help you fabricate an incident. Pay attention to current events, local news reports, newspapers, magazines, blogs etc. about real people involved in real situations and morph these stories to fit your screenplay. Read history books. Deep in their pages you'll find dynamic incidents that caused furors or social upheaval and affected lives. But that doesn't mean that you've got to write period pieces.

You can morph those historical events into modern ones by finding current parallels. Since history tends to repeat itself, there are situations occurring today that may not be too far off what happened years before. Certainly they will have changed to allow for current mind-sets—often growing more subtle perhaps, but they still create problems for people and you can use them to create compelling social issue stories relevant today. For instance, people lost their homes in the Great Depression and they are losing them again now as the mortgage bubble bursts.

Make sure though, that your story isn't based on incorrect notions of what you *imagine* the social issue is all about. Unfortunately, some screenwriters, blinded by their altruism, make the mistake of creating screenplays about issues they portray inaccurately, fantastically, or just plain incorrectly. For example, one semester I taught a course in which students were asked to write screenplays for social issue movies that they ended up actually making in the following semester. The students came in and chose a social issue that interested them. These issues ranged from homelessness to domestic violence. Then, the students wrote outlines for short films about their issues. After discussing and workshopping the outlines, the students went out into the community and spent several weeks volunteering at venues where they could learn about these social issues. They worked at homeless shelters, domestic abuse safe houses, gang rehabilitation centers and other social agencies.

When they came back they were asked to revise their outlines and after their experiences with reality, the students came back with radically different stories. They all realized that they had idealized, fantasized, and imagined their social issues and that the reality they experienced when confronting these issues was radically different from their initial suppositions.

To make sure that you've got the right handle on the issue you choose and that you are being realistic and accurate, you might want to immerse yourself in that issue by volunteering or performing community service. And while you're doing that, you can garner valuable scenarios and facts. But don't be satisfied with superficial facts. Look a little deeper into those facts to find details you can spin into broader or more dynamic stories. Sometimes the not-so-obvious stories behind the facts are more interesting.

Here's an example from my own life. I was a naive nineteen-year-old cub reporter working on what was then Canada's largest newspaper, the *Toronto Star*. I got an assignment to cover a story about an important and expensive hospital development scheduled to be built in a populated downtown area. My editor told me that the facts were simple: the hospital would create much-needed employment, serve a currently unserved portion of the urban population and be a boon to local business. I was told to get neighborhood reaction to this perceived urban "blessing."

Wearing my best reporter's outfit (red suit, black hat, big-lady high-heeled shoes—hooked on old movies even then, I wanted to be Hildy Johnson in *His Girl Friday!*) and made my way to the proposed site. The houses in that neighborhood were all older modest attached row houses with joyful little gardens in front. I knocked on a random door. A middle-aged man wearing a wife-beater and suspenders, opened the door. When I told him that I was from *The Toronto Star* and wanted to ask him about the new hospital, his face lit up. He ushered me into his small kitchen and while I waited made several phone calls in broken English to his neighbors. I thought I had struck pay dirt. I wouldn't have to knock on scads of doors and could get all the quotes I needed.

When nearly a dozen neighbors arrived—Italian, Armenian and Portuguese immigrants who could barely speak English—I quickly discovered that they were vehemently opposed to the hospital going in because it meant they would all lose their homes. Some of these people cried. Others shouted. But all of them were emotional about how much their hard-won homes meant to them and how bitterly they resented their proposed loss.

I tried to reassure them by reminding them that they would be compensated by the developer but they told me that the small amount of money offered wouldn't allow them to buy homes in that current housing market. They were devastated and desperate. They asked me for help, and because of my own immigrant past, I could relate to them on a personal level and was inspired to write a story about their plight and what the development would mean for that community of newcomers. I assured them that my story could create a public outcry that might prevent the development from going forward.

I listened to each person's story and made notes. I went back to the newspaper and began my research. Because there was no internet at the time (hard to imagine now!) I used methods that still work today. I made phone calls to city officials and to the development company and scoured the newspaper "morgue" for historical information about the neighborhood. I researched the extent to which developments had made inroads into communities throughout the country and the toll these developments have had on poor households. I researched house prices and discovered that the immigrants were correct in their belief they wouldn't be able to get new homes. I researched how children would be affected by the move to different school districts that were not as good and what the vacancy rate was in that area for rentals. I worked my heart out and stayed up all night.

I was proud of the story I wrote, but when I presented it to the city desk the next morning, I was dressed down and told that I hadn't done my job. The editors didn't want the story I told. They wanted a pro-development story that would paint the developers as community saviors bringing new jobs and state of the art medical care to the area. They didn't want to hear about the immigrants and their precious homes. Of course the fact that the development company consistently bought huge amounts of print advertising from the paper might have had something to do with why my story was spiked.

I was devastated and felt that I'd let the neighborhood down but nevertheless, from writing my version of that assignment, I learned that the "obvious" story based on the upfront facts about an issue may not be the story most worth telling. The better story—the story I wished the editors had approved—was the story with more emotional wallop and with more human interest. It was the story behind the facts.

Thinking of it in movie terms—the editor's story about the development has no real punch or verve. There's not much tension or conflict in it. It has "no legs." But my story, because of its emotional punch, has real movie potential.

To demonstrate how, let's develop a fictional story based on my old assignment. Let's imagine that a huge medical complex is being built in a close-knit urban neighborhood. A cub reporter (for romantic interest she's dating the son of one of the people living in the neighborhood) finds out from her boyfriend that the neighbors have been given inadequate compensation for their homes and have refused to sell them. The reporter is urged by her boyfriend's father and his friends to try and stop the development by making their stories public.

Even though editors refuse to consider running such a story, the reporter sides with her boyfriend and tries to come up with some strong reasons why the development shouldn't be built. She begins digging and ultimately discovers (and the audience with her) that the developer is dishonest and has an ulterior motive. He's in cahoots with the mayor and a group of councilmen who expect to get huge kickbacks from Mafia construction racketeers in exchange for building contracts.

The reporter tries to stop the development with the help of the neighborhood in spite of the opposition of her paper and comes up against corrupt journalism in the aid of corrupt big business, corrupt politicians and the corrupt mob. Does she save the day and stop the development or end up jobless and/or dead in a ditch? It depends on what we want to say about corruption, homeowners' rights and city politics. Do the rich guys always win or can they be stopped? How and at what cost?

Interesting Things To Consider In Writing A Movie

There's lots of "B" story (sub-plot) to play with here too: the editor trying to save his struggling paper gives in to pressure from corrupt developers who throw money at him; the boyfriend angle (many ways to go here—she could start out with him or she could meet him in the course of her investigations); the mayor and the developer in cahoots because perhaps they've discovered that there are rich mineral deposits under the neighborhood and have no intention of building the hospital at all but are simply appropriating the land and exploiting it, thereby crossing the Mafia! So many options and ways to go here! What a goldmine!

The personal elements of my own life experience made the story more "real" and vital for me. If I were ever to write that movie, my main inspiration and commitment to the issue would come from personal experience that I would combine *with* research—real facts about actual corporate and political corruption that have taken place in the past. The story I'd come up with doesn't have to be true, but can be used as a vehicle to make a point about corporate greed and corruption. I would use research to flush out the intricate details of the process but ultimately, the story would hinge on characters reacting to very real and huge obstacles.

Now let's outline the first act of my cub reporter vs developers unwritten screenplay (in the Investigator/Whistleblower Model) indicating where research is necessary to move forward.

Act One

1. Introduction of main character (Karen) and her job.
    Introduction of newspaper editor and his "problems."
    Paper in financial trouble
    (Research how newspapers are financed)
2. Introduction of Karen's boyfriend Alex and his family.
    Karen finds out that Alex's family and neighbors are going to lose their homes. (*Page 10 hook*)
    (Research how developers buy out neighborhoods)
3. Alex's father turns up dead in a mysterious "accident." *(Inciting Incident page 15)*
4. Karen tells her editor that she suspects something "fishy" because Alex's father was stalling the development by refusing to sell his house.
    The editor tells Karen to drop the story if she wants to keep her job.
    Meanwhile, the Mayor is nervous and upset. He's just had some tough, ugly visitors *(Subplot)*.
5. Alex's father's funeral.
    City officials and the developer show up at the funeral.

Alex confronts them in an emotional tirade.

As Karen calms him down, he tells her he is suspicious of the developers.

Outside the funeral home, the mayor and the developer have a conversation *(Subplot)*.

6. Karen and Alex are having breakfast in Alex's apartment.

An incendiary device is hurled through the front window.

Alex and Karen get out of the apartment before it explodes.

Karen determines to investigate even if it means her job.

(End of Act One. Page 30!)

I've made this story fairly simple so you can see how much actual writing can be done with a small amount of research. In the next section of the script (Act Two: Plot points 7–18) most of the research will come into play. For example, the next part of your outline might look like this.

Act Two

7. Karen researches the developer. *(Research developers and their finances.)*

8. Alex finds out something about city zoning laws. *(Research how zoning laws are made.)*

He gets the runaround from City Hall *(Subplot)*. *(Research city hall bureaucracy.)*

9. The mayor gets City Council to change the zoning laws. *(Research how to do this.)*

The neighbors form a group to protest. *(Involves subplot and main plot.)*

(Page 45, First spike in the Second Act.)

And so on. As the story develops, you can do the research to flush out the outline and even write the first draft while you're researching. Remember, the characters, their reactions and relate-ability are more important than exposition. Obviously you want audiences to understand the issue so that information is necessary, but you also want them to connect emotionally to your characters in their struggles with the issue. The more subtle the exposition and the more compelling the character, the better the issue comes across. Find the emotional backbone and the compelling tension of your story before you flush out the expository details!

For emphasis, let's look at the first act outline of *Casablanca* again. This outline (certainly its main points) could have been written after some preliminary research about World War II Casablanca. Since the movie was written during that war, the events would have been current and the screenwriters (over thirty worked on this movie although Julius J. Epstein, Philip G. Epstein and Howard Koch are the only ones credited) included that research in the first plot point. It served to inform the audience but you can see how the details might have given rise to the story itself.

Casablanca First Act Outline

  1. **Intro of Casablanca** *(One minute)* *(Research required)*
      Opening history, info, background of time and era.

(Notice how the research material is presented at the top of the film to orient the audience and give background. It's brief and succinct but provides a lot of information.)

"FADE IN:

INSERT A revolving globe. When it stops revolving it turns briefly into a contour map of Europe, then into a flat map.

Superimposed over this map are scenes of refugees fleeing from all sections of Europe by foot, wagon, auto and boat, and all converging upon one point on the tip of Africa—Casablanca.

Arrows on the map illustrate the routes taken as the voice of a NARRATOR describes the migration.

NARRATOR (VO)

With the coming of the Second World War many
eyes in imprisoned Europe turned hopefully or
desperately, toward the freedom of the Americas.
Lisbon became the great embarkation point. But not
everybody could get to Lisbon directly, and so, a
tortuous, roundabout refugee trail sprang up. Paris,

NARRATOR (VO) continued

Marseilles, across the Mediterranean to Oran, then
by train, or auto, or foot, across the rim of Africa to
Casablanca in French Morocco. Here, the fortunate
ones, through money, or influence, or luck, might
obtain exit visas and scurry to Lisbon and from
Lisbon to the New World. But the others wait in
Casablanca—And wait—and wait—and wait."[1]

*(The information is made visual in an extension of the first plot point. Now
the rest of the movie can be written without too much blatant exposition.
The exposition that's needed often comes in dialogue.)*

1. B. *Intro of atmosphere, politics, issues, minor characters (Four
   minutes)*
   - description/depiction of political climate (research required)
   - intro of young couple (visual)
   - intro of underground and importance of papers (research
     required)
   - intro of some minor running characters (pickpocket)
   - intro of Major Strasse and Col. Renault
   - verbal intro of Rick.
2. *Intro of Sam, Rick, Letters of transit (Five minutes)*
   - intro of Rick's place as hub of planning and scheming to
     get away
   - Intro of Sam
   - intro of workers, gambling and Rick's policies
   - intro of Rick himself and his character traits
   - intro of Ugati
   - Ugati is established as a killer while Rick is principled
   - Ugati gives Rick letters of Transit. (Page ten hook.)
3. *Relationships, characters, information (Seven minutes)*
   - Rick hides letters
   - Introduction of Ferrari (Sydney Greenstreet) and Blue
     Parrot
   - Yvonne and Sasha introduced
     —Rick's attitude toward women

- Relationship between Rick and Renault
- Rick's past
- Victor Laszlo talked about. (He'll want the letters of transit and he's important.)

4. *The Arrest of Ugati (Five minutes)*
   - Renault and Strasse
   - Establish Rick as ruthless re Ugati
   - Rick and Germans
   - More Laszlo information.

5. *Laszlo appears (Five minutes)*
   - Laszlo and Elsa introduced
   - existence of Underground established
   - Elsa recognizes Sam, Rick.

6. *Elsa and Rick (Three minutes)*
   - their eyes meet, they have history.

7. *End of Act. Page 28 with three-page transition*
   - Rick is drinking and for the first time, vulnerable (p. 31).

Notice that only a small amount of research was required just to get into Act One. The rest of the story could be written with some research filling in the holes regarding the operation of the Nazis in occupied France and their methods in general. That's because Casablanca fits into the Relationship Model even though it's got elements of the Shining Armor Model.

These examples demonstrate that you can start writing immediately, setting up the characters and the premise in Act One and then, when you hit a hole in information, you can research that particular aspect. This "all at once" method makes your research more focused, more character and plot oriented and specific, and prevents you from getting swamped by details and overwhelmed by facts that may not be directly pertinent or useable in your screenplay.

When you're ready to do research you'll need to use the techniques of good journalism.

Here are some basic ground rules. Let's use the Academy Award Winning Screenplay *Juno* (a teenager becomes pregnant and decides against abortion in favor of adoption) as an example of their application.

If you use the internet (and you probably will at first) make sure that you corroborate every fact. The internet tends to become a little murky when accuracy is concerned, so it's your job if you want to get the facts right, to back everything up with a second credible source.

For example, in order to come up with a story about a pregnant teenager (*Juno*) you can Google "teenage pregnancy" and among the sources you'll find the Guttmacher Institute—a foundation that receives major grants from The William and Flora Hewlett Foundation, the David and Lucile Packard Foundation and the Ford Foundation. The institute publishes papers by reputable scholars. These papers include facts and statistics about teenage pregnancy and abortion rates in the U.S. Because these scholars always quote their references, you can be sure that the information provided is correct. If you were "researching" a story like *Juno*, you could go to this source to learn facts about abortion and teenage pregnancy that will inform your screenplay vis-à-vis how teenagers have access to abortions and their attitudes toward it.

PAY ATTENTION TO FACTS AND MAKE STATISTICS "REAL"

Pay attention to all the facts even though they may seem contradictory and be careful about statistics. They can seem meaningless. What is more dramatic is the real story behind the statistics. Numbers are impersonal and it's your job as a screenwriter to make them real by making them personal. Attach them to characters or situations audiences can relate to.

For example, The Guttmacher Institute says that "in repeated studies since the early 1980s, leading experts have concluded that abortion does not pose a hazard to women's mental health."[2] And yet, the *Medical Science Monitor* of October 2004 says that "64% of women who experienced one or more abortions 'felt pressured by others' to have this abortion."

It's obvious to me that a woman feeling pressured might be in a high state of anxiety and that might pose a hazard to her mental health. Here we've got a statistic and contradictory facts that can provide some interesting scenes in a movie about teenage pregnancy.

When Juno finds out she's pregnant, her knee-jerk reaction is to get an abortion—particularly since she sees a large newspaper ad depicting a distraught Teen girl clutching her head in a moment of staged conflict. The ad reads: "Pregnant? Find the clinic that gives women choice. Women's Choice Health Center."[3] It just seems like the thing to do—a definite social pressure.

But when Juno approaches the abortion clinic she finds her classmate holding a sign that reads "No Babies Like Murdering" and chanting "All Babies want to be Borned." Juno stops to talk and some very clever expository writing reveals that she's had mental issues in the past.

> **JUNO**
> Uh, hi, Su-Chin
>
> **SU-CHIN**
> Oh, hi Juno. How are you?
>
> **JUNO**
> Good. I'm good.
> (Pause)
> Did you finish that paper for Worth's class yet?
>
> **SU CHIN**
> No, not yet. I tried to work on it a little last night but I'm having trouble concentrating.
>
> **JUNO**
> You should try Adderall.
>
> **SU-CHIN**
> No thanks. I'm off pills.
>
> **JUNO**
> Wise move. I know this girl who had a huge crazy freakout because she took too many behavioral meds at once. She took off her clothes and jumped into the

> **JUNO** (Cnt'd)
> fountain at Ridgedale Mall and she was like,
> "Blaaaaah! I'm a kraken from the sea!"
>
> **SU-CHIN**
> I heard that was you.[4]

In the light of her past mental health history the audience understands why Juno might feel she's not ready to be a parent. Her history and society's public acceptance of abortion initially "pressures" Juno to quickly decide to abort. In spite of this, Juno decides, almost just as quickly, against abortion. Again, she's "pressured" by Su-Chin's comments:

> **SU-CHIN**
> Your baby probably has a beating heart, you know. It
> can feel pain. And it has fingernails.
>
> **JUNO**
> Really? Fingernails?

She considers the concept, then pushes open the clinic door.[5]

The audience can see the idea sinking in when Juno takes a seat in the waiting room.

Then she looks over and notices the FINGERNAILS of a nearby teen, who looks as nervous as she does. The girl bites her thumbnail and spits it onto the floor.

Juno looks away, but immediately notices another waiting woman who absently scratches her arm with long fake nails.

Suddenly, she sees fingernails EVERYWHERE. The receptionist clicks her nails on the front desk, Another woman blows on her fresh manicure. Everyone seems to be fidgeting with their fingers somehow.

Juno suddenly looks terror stricken.[6]

This scene reinforces the "pressure" Juno feels in deciding to abort or not to abort. In this way "research" about pressure and mental health can inform the screenplay in a subtle and effective way as can research on fetus development and abortion clinic protocol.

In order to do this, you'll need to research and examine the "process" of your issue. In *Juno*, the audience was taken from conception, to pregnancy test, to Juno's relationship with the unborn child's father, to abortion, to deciding against abortion, to deciding to adopt, to telling parents, to searching out and meeting adoptive parents, to struggling with the realities of the adoptive parents, to struggling with the relationship and to ultimately giving up the child and resolving the relationship. The process is clear and believable and without knowing that process (researching it), the screenwriter could not have taken us on that journey. Screenwriter Cody could, for instance have looked at the statistics and information about Teen Pregnancy on the Centers for Disease Control website[7] as well, and about fetal development[8] on various websites and in books and about adoption[9] but her research didn't overwhelm her story.

Instead, she was able to use it to create a wonderful journey taken by an engaging character. Making up a character like Juno to experience teenage pregnancy and talk about abortion and adoption is very effective. Because Juno (the character) is so likeable, smart, funny, headstrong and brave the audience takes her to heart and completely understands the issue she's involved in and why she makes the choices she does. Even those who are strongly pro-abortion can find themselves understanding and ultimately agreeing with Juno's decision to have her child and give it away because they are able to follow her through the process which seems real and sincere to them and rings true.

Ultimately, *Juno* is a social issue movie about teenage pregnancy, abortion and adoption. Yet it isn't tedious or preachy. In fact, because it showcases the character and her experiences with the issue at its every stage, it makes for compelling watching and can provoke much thought and discussion. There are those that call it a Pro-Life, Pro-Adoption movie and yet, because of the Juno character herself, audiences without those proclivities can enjoy the movie for its wit, charm and good nature.

The social issue movies that work best are not those filled with facts and statistics but those whose characters confront "facts" in an interesting, reality-based and often soul-wrenching way. Since we live in a culture of sound bites and "quick-shock-overwhelm," facts themselves, even if they are amazing, don't have the power to capture audience attention for two hours unless they are embedded in stories that involve engaging characters.

In your research you need to look for examples of characters that you can develop and through which you can tell your story. These characters need to inspire you, move you and engage audiences. Ultimately, as has already been said, no matter how much research you do and no matter how accurate your movie is, it will fall flat unless you have engaging and strongly drawn characters that will take audiences into the issue with them.

No matter what, don't let yourself be intimidated by research. Don't let it delay your writing. Remember, while the information about a social issue might be what you want people to know, it's the way you present it that will inspire them to care.

We've just seen how a small amount of selective research on abortion, teen pregnancy and adoption, could have been used in *Juno*. Following, are three examples of brief research information on three social issues. To illustrate my point, I've come up with two story ideas for each issue based on that research.

Choose two or three social issues that interest you, do some brief research and come up with at least two story ideas for each. As I've done, try to come up with story ideas that aren't obvious. At the end of this exercise, you should have material for several screenplays.

Brief Research Information On Social Issues

Censorship

> "*Supreme Court Rules to Allow Censorship in High Schools.* While stating that student speech should be protected, The Supreme Court ruled 5–4 to limit those rights after a high school senior was suspended for displaying a sign with a drug reference at a school-sponsored activity."[10]

Obvious story idea: A high school student writes an inflammatory article in the school paper, is suspended for it and fights for his rights of free speech in court. (I'd use *The Lawyer-Up* and feature an ambitious new lawyer.)

Not so obvious: An evil high school teacher manipulates a student into an affair by using the new censorship law in a creative way. Her friends find out and band together to punish the teacher in creative ways. (I'd use *The Chuckle* and write this as a comedy.)

Civil rights

"A recent national survey sponsored by the Brennan Center for Justice at NYU School of Law reveals that millions of American citizens do not have readily available documentary proof of citizenship. Many more—primarily women—do not have proof of citizenship with their current name. The survey also showed that millions of American citizens don't have government-issued photo-identification, such as a driver's license or passport. Finally, the survey demonstrated that certain groups—primarily poor, elderly and minority citizens—are less likely to possess these forms of documentation than the general population."[11]

Obvious idea: A mother of three, who is an American citizen, is stopped by ICE, and because she has no identification, she's deported to her native country—a place where she's in terrible danger. Her husband, who's illegal, risks everything to get her back into the States to save her life. (I'd use The Shining Knight and make the husband a hero.)

Not so obvious: An ICE agent falls in love with a woman he suspects is an illegal immigrant, keeps quiet about it and then rues the day when she ends up assassinating a prominent government official. (I'd use The Heart-Tugger and focus on the relationship between the couple that ends in the ultimate betrayal.)

Education

"Students at risk of not successfully completing their high school educations indicate that their arts participation motivates them to stay in school, and that the arts create a supportive environment that promotes constructive acceptance of criticism and one in which it is also safe to take risks."

"With music in schools, students connect to each other better—greater camaraderie, fewer fights, less racism and reduced use of hurtful sarcasm."[12]

Obvious idea: An edgy high school student, often truant and into drugs, discovers that his love of music can take him where he only dreamed of going. (I'd use The Yoda and give him a mentor who's an old blues musician.)

Not so obvious: A gang member steps outside his "family" and risks his life to make contact with a kid from another gang whose musical ability he envies. (I'd use *The Heart-Tugger* to focus on the relationship between the gang members.)

9
GETTING IT MADE

Screenwriters believe it's not their job to sell a movie. That's what agents are for. Or are they? It's an agent's job to promote, push and introduce your work to production companies and studios, but getting a movie made takes more than that. It's a grueling and frankly impossible process and it's the hardest thing going. Even Academy Award winning screenwriter and director Brian Helgeland, speaking at a forum at Loyola Marymount University, said it was impossible. So if you're a screenwriter and passionate about getting the word out on a social issue and you've got a great screenplay, what do you do?

First, let's assume you don't have an agent. Getting one is almost as difficult as getting a movie made. That's because thousands of people around the country are constantly bombarding agents with projects that may or may not be movie worthy. Lots of people everywhere believe they've got great movie stories and some of them even try to write screenplays. For instance, a while back I was checking in a rental car at a mid-western airport when the guy doing the paperwork found out that I lived in Los Angeles. Suddenly he started pitching me his screenplay. I could have been an insurance salesman for all he knew, but because I was living where Hollywood was, he assumed I'd spark to his project and catapult him to success.

That happens a lot in Los Angeles. I've had saleswomen at department stores pitch me ideas as they walked me to a fitting room, car jockeys pitching me as they brought back my car and even a vet ignored my sick dog, and started giving me details about the "fabulous script" he'd written. He was so distracted that he misdiagnosed my dog and she died. The next day he called to tell me he was sorry and then suggested that we "do" lunch so we could talk more about his script! I was disgusted.

If this kind of stuff happens to me—a writer—you can imagine how many come-ons agents get. It becomes difficult to sort out the great from the criminally crappy. That's why agents hire readers— fledgling wannabe screenwriters who read submitted screenplays and write coverage on them. (Coverage includes a synopsis of the story, its' strengths, weakness and whether the agent should bother reading it.) Who are these readers? Usually they are interns culled from film schools all around Los Angeles. And what qualifications do these interns have? None at all save that they are enrolled in a university and are willing to work for free. Some of my first-year students who have had no experience whatsoever with writing or screenplay analysis are doing coverage at agencies and yes, at production companies where scripts submitted by agents are sent. In fact, some people doing coverage aren't even students. I know of one film executive who gives his twenty-something pool boy scripts to read because he's from the right demographic. It's all cruel and somehow absurd isn't it? But it's the process that's in play.

Of course there are ways of getting around the process. If you know someone who's an agent, married or related to an agent or sleeping with an agent (or you yourself know an agent in any of these capacities) then you may be fortunate enough to be taken on. But only if your work won't embarrass the agent. Someone who knows and likes you can still back away from your project if it threatens his own credibility. It's a business after all and agents put business first.

If you aren't lucky enough to be connected in some way to agent-land, then your best bet is to get hold of the list of agents who are signatories to the Writer's Guild and write them all query letters. A good query letter is short (no more than one page or less if you can swing it) and gives a punchy tag line to your project and some information about you. The best way to start one of these letters and interest the agent's assistant who will pass the letter on or dump it if it isn't great, is to talk about the rights you have to a book or true story. If you have that, it may be easier to get a reading by, or even a meeting with, the agent.

You can start your letter by saying something like:

"Sixteen years ago, Ellen's husband Larry ran off with another man. The only problem was, the other man was a spy for the KGB and Larry was a secret service agent working for the President." That's a true story and I've got the rights to Ellen's life-story. Would you be interested in reading the screenplay? I'm looking for representation and hope very much that you spark to my work."

Next, briefly list your qualifications and credits. If you aren't a screenwriter and have no credits, you might just want to say nothing more. Or you can pull an "I'm so unusual" card and tell them that you're a welder living in Portland (or whatever else you do) who's related to Ellen. Keep in mind though, that if you have no screenwriting abilities or chops, you might just get left in the dust even though you have the rights. The agent might want to take you on just to peddle the rights and then have you thrown off the project (always a possibility). If that does happen, you'd be able to bargain for a credit and get some money out of it and that wouldn't be bad at all. You will have made a little headway into Hollywood and had a great start.

Make sure you don't start your query with some altruistic statement the agent may not spark to. For example, don't begin with "haven't you always wanted to help the homeless?" The agent may have a particular beef against the homeless and will read no further. I found that out the hard way. This actually happened to me although it's hard to believe. I once opened a pitch to a production executive with the words "This is a story about the triumph of the human spirit." The exec stopped me and snarled, "I don't care about the human spirit, I want a project with sex and violence."

My pitch was over and so was my relationship with that exec. Who wants to work with someone like that? So be careful to start your query (or your face-to-face pitch if you're lucky enough to get one) with a statement that will arouse interest and curiosity about the story itself. Please know that no matter how great your query letter may be, the return on agent solicitation is usually less than one percent. I know people who've sent out fifty letters and received only one response. That's pretty good and if that happens to you, you should rejoice.

An alternative, if you have the rights to something great, is to go directly to a production company where a development person may see you to hear your pitch. But remember that you'll probably be thrown off the project and given a minimal credit because the production company, trolling for good ideas, will want to use its own people rather than someone they don't know who has no track record. In those cases, you will have to see what kind of deal the company will offer you to get the rights away from you. That's when you'll need to get a lawyer, or you could use that deal in play to get an agent.

You can simply call an agent, tell him/her that you've got a deal pending with a production company and need someone to negotiate it for you. Agents won't turn down such easy money (they get 10 to 15 percent don't forget) and will often take you on for that one project. Once they do that, it will be your job to convince them you've got other deals that are just as good.

If you are lucky enough to get a face-to-face pitch meeting (and your story or book has to be really compelling, timely or sensational to get you that far) remember that pitching is a difficult and arduous process and there are lots of ways to go about it. It's an art and it depends on how great a storyteller and actor you are.

In a pitch, as in a query letter, keep it simple, scintillating and to the point. Make people want to know more about the story. And don't forget, you want to *sell* the story, not necessarily *tell* the story. Don't go on and on at great length. If they want to know more, they'll have to read your screenplay. You can't be shy or quiet. You've got to put your story out there and get them hooked.

If you don't have the rights to anyone's story or to a book, then the next thing you might want to try is to get an actor or director involved in your project and attached to it. This isn't easy but it can be done. Let's say you're involved in an issue that has an organization behind it. And suppose that the organization has an actor involved who's interested in that issue. You could approach that person and pitch your project and see if he/she bites. Something like that happened with *Trust*, the 2010 David Schwimmer project.

David Schwimmer gained fame and fortune playing Ross Geller on the successful sitcom *Friends*. When he was on that show, the Rape

Treatment Center in Santa Monica, California approached him about making a public service announcement about date rape. It happened to be an issue Mr. Schwimmer was familiar with. He says, "Several of my friends have been victims of date rape and child sexual abuse, and a girlfriend of mine was a victim of both."[1]

Soon Schwimmer joined the board of directors of the center. Eventually he decided to make a movie about a teenage girl who becomes the victim of an online sexual predator. "He hired two screenwriters (Robert Festinger and Andy Belin) to develop a script based on interview transcripts and video recordings of victims and predators. They sat in as an F.B.I agent posed as an under-age target in online chat rooms. 'Every single line in the script was run past counselors,' Mr. Schwimmer said."[2]

Even so, the film was conceived as a thriller and not a preachy sermon. "The first job is to entertain and move people," he said, "so every cut I had to strip away more and more advocacy—little pieces of dialogue where it was an important fact but it was slowing down the scene or taking you out of it to the point where you suddenly think, 'What am I watching? 60 Minutes.'"[3]

Based on the script and his passion for the project, Schwimmer was able to bring the actor Clive Owen on board. His addition strengthened the package so much that the small independent Millennium Films (whose films include *The Expendables*) agreed to finance the film. It was released in the spring of 2011 but unfortunately didn't get wide distribution.

So even though a film may get made, getting it distributed is a whole other story. For example, one of my former students Monty Lapica made the fabulous feature film *Self-Medicated* (2005) based on his own life about a drug rehab boot camp for teenagers. He raised an estimated $500,000 to make it and wrote, directed, and starred in it. The film won *thirty* national and international awards including the Grand Jury Prize at the Rome Independent Film Festival, the Best Film Award at the Australian International Film Festival, the 2006 Prism Award and the 2007 Angel Award. In spite of that, hardly anyone saw it because it didn't get wide distribution.

That's probably because the film contained a few very pointed and heavy Christian/God references but was gritty and graphic. That meant it might have been too intense for Christian film distributors and too Christian for general distributors.

After I saw a cut, I suggested to Monty that he might want to trim the "in-your-face" religious stuff. He refused to change anything. He was determined to say what he wanted to say even though it might hurt him. I admired his integrity.

Unfortunately, in order to get distribution, it's essential to play to general audiences in some way and sometimes, people who make social issue movies who want to make blatant statements and express strong opinions have problems with that. You may want to think about how much you're willing to compromise if you are determined to raise money for your film and make it yourself. Raising money isn't easy. Try and borrow a few bucks from a near stranger and see how that goes. But it can be done if you are determined.

You can write a script that is very low budget with minimal locations and if you shoot digitally, forsaking film, you can make a feature for very little money. A few of my students have done that—one made a feature for $75,000 and two others for $10,000 and even though the production values weren't great, at least they got their movies made and into festivals. Unfortunately they didn't get much traction.

Also, you've got to be careful that you don't have to give back the money you've raised. Some people looking for tax shelters may be able to give you money based on your social issue film as a "donation" and reap tax credits that way. You can also set up a non-profit to which people can give money, but that might present a problem if your film makes money and you're not putting it into a non-profit of some sort. You'll need a savvy tax attorney to help you figure it all out.

Of course grants are always a possibility. One of my students got money to fund his short film on teenage suicide by getting a grant from a suicide prevention organization who wanted to use the film for educational purposes. There are all kinds of creative ways to raise money for films. Make sure you consult accountants and lawyers before you start soliciting funds.

Certainly, you'll need to make sure that people who want to put up money for your film don't have ulterior motives. For example, you might be cajoled into casting someone's disastrously untalented stage-struck daughter/wife/mistress as the star of your film in exchange for some considerable cash. While this cash could help your film to get made, that kind of casting could sink it. You also want to make sure that investors don't get any creative control. The consortium of dentists who might give you lots of financial backing, shouldn't show up on the set to suggest your movie needs more shots of teeth! These things do happen and once they start, they snowball, because everyone who shells out cash ultimately believes they should have a say in how it's spent.

In my first movie, because the distributor (a cigar smoking guy named Murray) put up half the money for the film, he got a creative say. After we screened the film for him, he turned to his son and wife who were watching the final cut with us, and asked them what they thought. They made a face and said they thought the opening was too long. He grabbed a pair of scissors lying nearby and stood up, saying he was just going to cut the first few "sections" out of the print. We were horrified and promised to cut it ourselves. And we did. Murray must have been right because that film (*Home Free*) won all kinds of awards (which Murray kept) and eventually was distributed in schools by Pyramid Films and played on Showtime.

The hope is, of course, that if you can get your movie into a festival and do well, you can get picked up by a company that will either take your film as it is or re-shoot it. Think *Blair Witch Project* (1999) which was pieced together from shaky footage. The estimated budget was $60,000 and according to IMDB stats it has so far grossed $248,639,099! That's the dream that keeps independent film makers going.

No matter what you do though, please remember that there are lots of social issues you can explore and lots of screenplays you can write. Don't make the mistake of holding on to one social issue project for years and years. For example, I know a screenwriter who has written one social issue film he cares deeply about. He has spent twenty years flogging that script. Even though one of my mottos is: "Never Give Up!" I do believe you've got to know when to move on.

Even if you believe that you shouldn't abandon your project entirely, keep it in the wings while you write other things. If you are successful at writing other projects, you might eventually be able to sell that pet social issue script eventually. The key is to keep writing and creating other projects based on other issues you think are important. There's a whole world out there to fix!

Getting a movie made is really really hard, and you should know that before you get too down on yourself for not being able to do it quickly. Consider the thousands of people out there and the limited amount of resources available for film making. A screenplay is difficult to sell no matter what it's about, particularly in the present economy, where many companies are cutting staff and reducing the amount of product they put out.

Fortunately there are many other venues opening up for film makers. You can always shoot a short version of your project and get that into festivals. When that gets noticed, you can pull out your feature and entice companies that way. You can use your short film as a sizzle reel to let people know what to expect from your project. Keep in mind that a short film shouldn't be more than ten minutes long and should stand alone with a beginning, middle, and an end even though it's taken from the feature. If you can get the length down to five to eight minutes you're in good shape because festivals don't like to slot films much longer than that. If you shoot the project digitally, it shouldn't cost you more than about $3,000 if you're careful and get lots of people to work for free.

Of course there's always *YouTube* but that's a little problematic because there's no way to weed out the garbage from the gold. Because everything gets dumped on *YouTube*, your film, no matter how fabulous, can go missing and be ignored. While it's true that some production companies have interns trolling the web for do-able projects, finding one is like winning the lottery—but that doesn't mean it doesn't happen.

Studios have set up web divisions specifically for producing webisodes they can then morph into TV series. Some of them have even bought ideas from novices that they've found online. In 2009 I worked with some of my students on a project in conjunction with ABC Television's Stage Nine to create webisodes for a pilot web channel. One of my students got a project in the works but recently, Stage Nine was discontinued by Disney. There's not a lot of traction in the webisode market and certainly it hasn't proved successful in getting a feature made. Participant Media is talking about making short social issue films to play on a channel (Take Part TV) in the new *Google/*

YouTube platform but isn't sure where those films will come from. Nothing is up and running quite yet.

I don't want to sound pessimistic, but the realities of the business are often staggering. As a writer, you've got to decide what keeps you going. It should be a passion for your craft, your subject and your process. It should be the conviction that what you have to say is important and if you're willing to make sacrifices and work hard, if you're willing to pay your dues, get a day job and let nothing stand in your way, then you will be successful.

But you've got to decide what being successful means to you. You can consider yourself a success if you actually finish a social issue screenplay. You can consider yourself a success if you make every effort to sell it and if you've done your best doing that and made people aware of the issue in the process. The key thing to know is that success needs to be defined as an internal process and not always as an external one. I often go to Writer's Guild events and hear produced screenwriters who others consider successful, putting down their own work. Just because your work has been produced, doesn't mean it comes from a part of you that is vital and feeds your soul.

If you make a social issue film (even a short one), show it to people and it changes even one person's life or thinking about a social issue and gets that person motivated to contribute and make a difference, then you've been successful. And that's really something to acknowledge and applaud.

Making It: A Case Study

The Whistleblower (2010)
Written by: Eilis Kirwan and Larysa Kondracki
Directed by: Larysa Kondarcki
Starring: Rachel Weisz and Vanessa Redgrave
Social issue: Child abuse (human trafficking) and human rights (torture).

To illustrate all the points I've made in this section, let's look at *The Whistleblower*, a powerful and effective film about human trafficking. *The Whistleblower* is an independent feature with a relatively small budget (just under $8 million) made by first-time director Larysa

Kondracki and first-time writer Eilis Kirwan. It's the gripping and sometimes hard-to-watch true story of Nebraska cop Kathryn Bolkovac who, while working as a U.N. peacekeeper in Bosnia, uncovered the human trafficking of young girls facilitated by U.N. peacekeepers themselves. Here's how the movie got made according to co-writer Eilis Kirwan who I interviewed in October 2011.

In 1998, Kirwan came to the U.S. from Dublin, Ireland on a Fulbright scholarship to study directing. She had an undergraduate degree in English and History and had worked in Dublin as a playwright. "I had movies in the back of my mind," she said, "but what was accessible in the world that I lived in and what I knew I could do immediately was plays. I loved what I saw on the BBC and thought of writing for television as well as film."

She applied to NYU and Columbia to study either dramatic writing or film and eventually did enter the graduate film program at Columbia. She graduated as a director even though she wrote scripts as well and always identified herself as a writer. "If I had to choose," she said, "I'd choose writing You're more in control as a writer. You can always be creating. As a director you need money."

Two years later, she met Ukranian-Canadian Larysa Kondracki who had just come into the Columbia film program. In 2003, Kondracki was looking for a project to shoot as a feature for her thesis film. She had been inspired by Kimberly Pierce, also a Columbia student, who made *Boys Don't Cry* (1999) based on her short thesis film. Kondracki began to research human trafficking and found a book witten by a Canadian journalist Victor Malarek entitled *The Natashas: Inside the New Global Sex Trade* (Arcade Publishing, 2003). That book included a chapter on Kathryn Bolkovic and her activities in Bosnia. Once Kondracki found Bolkovic, she realized her name was all over the internet and the press in England and Europe but it just hadn't reached the U.S. She asked Kirwan, who had just graduated, to write the script with her and the project began.

Kondracki and her mother raised $30,000 from the Canadian-Ukranian community in Toronto to finance travel to research the project. Kondracki googled Bolkovic, found her address online and contacted her saying that she was a young film maker who found her story fascinating and inspiring. Bolkovic agreed to talk to her.

In October, 2004, Kondracki and Kirwan flew to Amsterdam where Bolkovic lives and spent the weekend with her and her husband. "By the end of the weekend," said Kirwan "we made our final plea telling her we didn't have any money but that we would do our absolute best and wouldn't give up to try and tell her story and get this thing out there. She said that she'd like to think if her daughters went out and asked for something like this, that someone would say yes to them." Since Kirwan and Kondracki reminded Bolkovic of her daughters she agreed to work with them.

The women got a lawyer and Bolkovic sold them her life rights for $100 against a final selling price to be determined. The option had to be renewed a few times before the film actually got made. That summer, Kondracki and Kirwan traveled to the Ukraine for research and then wrote the script. Kirwan said that they consulted with Bolkovic if they wanted to make big changes, but for the most part they kept to her story only compressing the back story and her life time-line slightly.

The story in Bosnia was compressed too and things were externalized that appeared in e mails or documents. It was also a great help that Bolkovic shared a perfect file of details and information. (A screenwriter's dream!) "She had evidence of everything and even tape recordings," said Kirwan. "We used some of them in actual speeches. Kathy did read the script a few times but had no objections to anything in it."

In 2005, when the script was finished, its log line appeared in a booklet Columbia University puts out for its' graduates called *Script Connect*. Producer Amy Kaufman, then the executive vice president of production at Focus Features (a specialty arm of Universal Features) liked the script and bought it. Kirwan and Kondracki were shocked. "It's not very often that Script Connect leads to something but I suppose it was just such an amazing story that it got noticed," said Kirwan.

Kondracki and Kirwan rewrote the script under Focus Features' auspices for about two years. But by then Focus had David Cronenberg's film *Eastern Promises* going into production. They said they couldn't do two films that covered the same ground so closely, so they put *The Whistleblower* into turnaround—essentially they dropped it.

Then HBO expressed interest in the screenplay and said they'd buy it for a new production company they were creating called Picture House to create films that would have a theatrical release. (That company no longer exists.) Kondracki and Kirwan developed (re-wrote) the script with HBO for about a year and a half. At that point, Colin Callender, who was the head of HBO at the time and the point person of the project, left the company. *The Whistleblower* was put into turnaround yet again.

It was an emotional roller coaster and the women got through it by working on other projects while shopping the screenplay around again. "*The Whistleblower* wasn't the only thing we were working on," said Kirwan. "In 2006 we moved to LA. We sold another pitch, got an assignment and we got an agent so that all helped us through it all."

"Getting an agent is not the key piece that people think it is," said Kirwan. "It's not the thing that gives you a career at all. I don't know if you ever know if you have a career. I don't necessarily think that I do. You still have periods when there is down time and you're not sure what's going to happen next. I feel very lucky because you can get caught up in all the machinations and anxiety.

"You have to understand hard work on the level that not everyone wants to deal with. If you want to write in a context where you're not just writing poetry or a one-woman show where it's a collaborative medium, you have to be open to having a creative conversation. My attitude to development executives is: 'Help me to understand what's not working for you in the script.' We always talk about the note behind the note. They might be saying what's wrong with it is different than the change that they want done. You've got to find out what the note behind the note is rather than get adversarial about what they are suggesting. Sometimes something's not working and no one knows why and the conversation can actually lead to the answer. In some ways it's just luck."

After HBO dropped the project, Amy Kaufman, who had left Focus Features to start her own company but who had stayed on as one of the producers of *The Whistleblower*, contacted Celine Rattray of Plum Pictures and brought her on board. Around that time, Rachel Weisz contacted Amy Kaufman (with whom she had made *The*

Constant Gardner—a 2005 film about corporate corruption) and asked about *The Whistleblower*.

"Rachel had read the script three years before through Amy at Focus," said Kirwan. "Rachel really liked the script but she was pregnant with her son and she felt that the darkness of the world was not a place where she could go at that time."

"And then later, just out of the blue, she rang up Amy and asked if that *Whistleblower* script was still around. Once Rachel was in position, the other cast members started falling into place. Rachel was at CAA and Vanessa Redgrave was at CAA and they just started sending the script around saying Rachel Weisz was in it."

"Once Rachel was on board, Telefilm Canada came forward with nearly $5 million and then Celine Ratray, a college friend of Larysa's who put together a co-production with a German colleague, got together the gap financing which was the final chunk of money needed."

All of those people participate in the film and they have a system of who gets first and second place. It's a little bit of a grab bag.

"There was still another little hurdle," said Kirwan. "There were some things Rachel wanted to develop about her character and exploring her character. She met Kathy on the set and not before because she didn't want to fall into the danger of doing an imitation. She just wanted to talk about motivation stuff. She's a very smart intelligent person and when I can tell that the person's goal is to make the film better that's fine with me. It was an interesting creative process to be discussing it with her. On the set with Vanessa (Redgrave) going through her lines was amazing and challenging and an incredible experience and was nearly all played as written."

"With Vanessa the discussion was more politically motivated than anything else. Part of her reason for getting involved in the film is that she feels very strongly about the mission of the United Nations as do I and she didn't want it to be a United Nations bashing sort of thing. She wanted to say that the reason this story is being told is because the United Nations is so important. We had material in the movie that expressed that sentiment."

"What was going on was a lot worse than what we showed in the movie. A guy came up and told Kathy that a girl he bought ran away and he thought that was ok to say that to the woman who was the head of gender affairs. So it just speaks to the cluelessness. We really pulled that stuff back but the story is what it is. They did look bad. But it doesn't mean that the entire mission of the UN is a bad thing."

The film played at the Toronto Film Festival and Samuel Goldwyn picked it up to distribute it and it's been playing widely—even in Lincoln, Nebraska where Bolkovic was a cop.

The Whistleblower took seven years to make and it was an exercise in perseverance and passion. And even though it exposed the social issue of human trafficking, it didn't put a stop to it. In fact, the ending of the film is rather hopeless. The UN peacekeepers who engaged in trafficking all had diplomatic immunity. The girl Bolkovic particularly tried to save was killed. Others never made it out. The ending was true to life and because *The Whistleblower* is an independent film, the writers didn't have to worry about altering the ending to make it "happier."

Eventually, for general distribution, they did have to cut some of the very graphic rape scene but they were amenable to that and agreed it should be re-cut. "I felt like in the end you really do have to tell what really happened to these women and so the real end of the story is what happens when people leave the theater," said Kirwan. "It's about a whistleblower and what is the action of a whistleblower? It's getting the truth out. People in audiences in a Q and A always ask 'What can we do?' in a kind of desperate rage and if it makes them do anything at all then that's great. Kathy has a website and she has links on it for action and there is legislation being proposed that is going to change the process of accountability for contractors at the UN."

"Before the film came out, there was a meeting at the UN with the Secretary General and the head of the Human Rights office and various other people and the discussion was on how to deal with this film. Larysa sent a letter and a DVD to the Secretary General and asked the UN to view it and have a discussion about it. He agreed."

In August of 2011, Kondracki got a letter from the Secretary General of the UN telling her that he had seen the film along with his senior advisers. He told her that the UN has reflected on the need to look seriously at the treatment of women and children in conflict situations. He also told her that the Security Council has taken certain steps and instigated key measures: the consolidation of several entities in the UN working on issues affecting women into UN Women; the appointment of the Special Representative of the Secretary-General on Sexual Violence in Conflict; and the strengthened mandates of the agencies such as the United Nations Office on Drugs and Crime and the Office of the High Commissioner on Human Rights.

He went on to say that "other pertinent internal reforms have also been taken to address directly the issue of sexual exploitation and abuse in the context of the United Nations peacekeeping operations."

He told her that Conduct and Discipline Units have been placed in each peacekeeping operation, a dialogue with Member States has established stricter standards for recruiting personnel and violations of codes of conduct are seriously followed up by the Heads of the Departments of Peacekeeping Operations and Field Service.

> The efforts of the Office of Investigation and Oversight Services as well as the Ombudsman have brought matters related to sexual abuse clearly within their official purview. Due protections are firmly in place for those who 'blow the whistle'.

He informed Kondracki that he had asked that a special screening of her film be arranged at the UN headquarters for staff and Member States with the full support of the President of the General Assembly and, as Kondracki suggested, he promised that there would be a panel discussion of the issues the film raises after the screening.[4]

In October 2011, the film was shown at the United Nations and a panel discussion was held that included Madeline Reiss (played by Redgrave in the film), Bolkovic's boss, an ex-human rights worker who worked at the UN and is working with Stanford University to put together a framework of how all this can be structured so that the people in the contractor system are not immune to prosecution.

Kondracki was also present and read a scathing statement denouncing the UN's claims of vigilance in stamping out human trafficking, saying that the measures put in place and sounding so effective, were not at all doing their job. She urged the UN to make apologies to and rehire whistleblowers who were dismissed for speaking out, and to put an end to the horrific abuses that are still continuing around the world. She noted that the same independent contracting firms responsible for the abuses detailed in the film are being re-hired again and again to act as peacekeepers and that not much has changed.

She was impressive and fearless and her statement and presence generated a very strong reaction from UN staff and the Member States. Kondracki noted in an email after the event, that the Prince of Jordan was extremely moved and expressed more than once the need to work on Member States' enforcement. The Secretary General's special representative on sexual violence in armed conflict (Margot Wollastrom) stated the UN should apologize both to victims and to Kathy Bolkovac. The discussion at the UN that day was recorded in its entirety.[5]

Kirwan and Kondracki are bowled over by the fact that this film is being talked about at the UN. Kirwan says:

> When we were on the streets in the Ukraine asking girls if they've ever heard of trafficking or when we were in underground shelters where they had trafficking victims did we ever think that the secretary general of the UN would be talking about this film? No, I don't think so. But deep down, the reason we did the film was that we did want to have an impact. We would have liked to copy the Participant model of outreach of their films but we didn't have the budget to do that.

And yet on a shoestring, with moxie, perseverance and a profound belief in the importance of their subject, two young women were able to get a film made that could eventually have a profound effect on the way UN Peacekeepers operate and that sheds light on a compelling and devastating social issue.

IT CAN BE DONE!!!

Afterglow

My teacher used to tell me "it's a great life if you don't weaken." It's easy to weaken. It's a tough world and there are all sorts of obstacles that make life "interesting." Screenwriters certainly have their share. That's because we're involved in a profession that's almost impossible to practice. We spend long hours alone working on visual stories that no one gets to see unless a whole mess of people agree to bring them to light and unless lots of money is available to do so. We suffer terrible rejections by strangers and even friends and family who may not like what we're doing and who may not understand our passion for doing it. We often have to make huge sacrifices to do our work—taking menial jobs to support our writing habit, working at things we don't like in order to squeeze out a few hours each week to write. We often spend more time disappointed than we do happy. We often feel unappreciated, misunderstood and ignored. Lots of times we have to watch less talented people achieve great success while we stand around with our hat in our hand, waiting for recognition that never comes. We have to beat down doors to get people to represent us and to believe in us and often they don't.

So why do we do it? What keeps us going? What's the thing we cling to in the stormiest waters and on the darkest days? It's the belief that we're doing something special and important that will somehow affect lives. We go on in spite of all the negatives because we believe profoundly that what we do can have some significance—can change and influence people even in small ways.

We do it for the love of the process, for the great thrill of discovering how people react to circumstances we conjure, and those of us who write social issue movies do it because we believe profoundly in our "cause" and that we can make the world a better place.

Every time we write a social issue movie we do it with belief. We believe the issue needs to be addressed and that what we're saying about it is important, essential and rare. And we enjoy saying it. We have a great time coming up with stories, characters, and events. We determine to experience real happiness in the act of writing and a feeling that we are valuable because we are doing valuable work. Using our movies to address social issues, no matter how small they may seem, is exciting, rewarding and highly valuable. Writing these kinds of movies gives us a great sense of satisfaction. It makes us feel good about ourselves. It makes us proud that we've taken on a difficult project and finessed it into a piece of art. That afterglow—the knowledge that we did our best, that we wrote with integrity and conscience, that we held to the truth, that our work is fine and good, and that it has a definite place in the world even if no one sees it, is what keeps us going. And really, that's all we have. No amount of money can replace it.

If we don't experience joy in writing and the sense that our work has value, nothing can make up for it. Even if we win awards, kudos, accolades, honors and scads of cash, if we don't have that inner bubble of joy going before, during and after the writing, we really haven't got anything. The glow of writing and the afterglow of having written well, bravely and honestly is what it's all about and why we keep on. The energy of that glow driving a social issue screenplay is what can truly light up and change the world.

Notes

Chapter 1

1. Yogananda, P. (1996). *Spiritual Diary*. Self-realization Fellowship, Los Angeles, CA. April 8 & 9.
2. Kennedy, R.F. (1993). *Collected Speeches*. New York: Viking Penguin, pp. 243–245.
3. Muggeridge, M. (1971). *Something Beautiful for God. Mother Teresa of Calcutta*. London: William Collins Sons and Co Ltd, p. 119.
4. Tutu, D. (2004). *God has a dream*. New York: Doubleday, p. 88.
5. King, M.L. Jr. (2007). *Conscience for Change. The lost Massey lectures*. Toronto: House of Anansi Press, p. 192.
6. Ibid., p. 211.
7. King, M.L. Jr. (1968). *I Have a Dream*. New York: Grosset and Dunlap, p. 2.
8. The Dalai Lama (2011). *How to be Compassionate*. New York: Atria Books, p. 10.
9. Ibid., p. 119.
10. Gates, B. (2011). *Annual Letter from the Bill and Melinda Gates Foundation*, p. 23.
11. Armstrong, K. (2011). *Peace Week Tele-Summit Keynote Speech*, September 18.
12. Leadingham, C., Moschella, J.E. & Vartanian, H.M. (Eds.) (1992). *Peace Prayers*. San Francisco: Harper Collins, p. 99.
13. Giri, Swami Sri Yukteswar (1990). *The Holy Science*. Self-realization Fellowship, Los Angeles, CA, p. 58.

Chapter 2

1. Malachi, 3:10, *The Holy Bible*, King James Version (1998). Grand Rapids, MI: World Publishing, p. 679.
2. Mata, Sri Daya (1999). *A World in Transition*. Self-realization Fellowship, Los Angeles, CA, p. 52.
3. Gould, S.J., Gupta, P.B. & Grabner-Krauter, S. (1997). Product placement in movies, *Journal of Current Issues and Research in Advertising*, *19*(1): 37–50.
4. Karniouchina, E.V., Uslay, C. & Erenburg, G. (2011). Do marketing media have life cycles? The case of product placement in movies, *Journal of Marketing*, *75*, 27–48.
5. *The American Heritage Dictionary*. (2006). Boston/New York: Houghton Mifflin Company, p. 1404.
6. Orwell, G. (2002). *Essays*. New York: Alfred A. Knopf, p. 352.
7. Beker, M. (2004). *Screenwriting with a Conscience: Ethics for screenwriters*. Mahwah, NJ: Lawrence Erlbaum Associates, p. 18.
8. Mallac, G. de (1989). *Gandhi's Seven Steps to Global Change*. Santa Fe, NM: Ocean Tree Books, p. 19.
9. Marcuse, H. (2007). *Art and Liberation. Collected papers, vol. 4*. London/New York: Routledge, p. 228.

Chapter 5

1. Leifermann, H.P. (1975). *Crystal Lee: A woman of inheritance*. New York: Macmillan.
2. *New York Times*, Philadelphia makers settle suit, March 20, 1966.
3. Simmons, A.M. (2001). Ex-skinhead seen as stereotype victim by his black lawyer, *Los Angeles Times*, August 1, Los Angeles, CA pp. AA1–2.

Chapter 6

1. Eliot, T.S. (1961). Burnt Norton. In Mack, Dean and Frost (Eds.) *Modern Poetry*. New York: Prentice Hall, p. 171.
2. Ebert, R. (1991). Oliver Stone defends JFK against conspiracy of dunces, *Chicago Sun Times*, December 22.
3. Harris, M. (2010). Inventing Facebook, *New York Magazine*, September 17.
4. Gardner, E. (2011). Judge may allow war veteran's bombshell lawsuit against 'Hurt Locker' to continue, *Hollywood Reporter*, August 9.

Chapter 7

1. *Backgrounder, Three Mile Island Accident*, U.S. NRC, Office of Public Affairs, nrc.gov.

Chapter 8

1. Epstein, Epstein, Kock. Casablanca. Warner Bros Pictures, 1942. p. 1.
2. Guttmacher Institute. Facts on Induced Abortion in the U.S. See www.guttmacher.org, January 2011.
3. Cody, D. (2007). *Juno. The Shooting Script*. New York: Newmarket Press, p. 31.
4. Ibid., p. 18.
5. Ibid., p. 19.
6. Ibid., p. 20.
7. See www.cdc.gov/vitalsigns/teenpregnancy/latestfindings.html.
8. See www.guttmacher.org.
9. See www.childwelfare.gov/adoption.
10. Finnegan, M. (2007). *Newshour Extra*. www.pbs.org, June 26.
11. Brennan Center for Justice at NYU School of Law (2006). Citizens without proof: A survey of American's possession of documentary proof of citizenship and photo identification, www.brennancenter.org.
12. See www.dosomething.org/tipsandtools/11-facts-about-music-education.

Chapter 9

1. *New York Times*, Directing trust is far from friends, March 27, 2011.
2. Ibid.
3. Ibid.
4. Moon, Ban Ki. Secretary General of the United Nations. Letter to Larysa Kondracki, August 11, 2011.
5. Available at: www.unmultimedia.org/tv/webcast/2011/10/panel-discussion-sexual-exploitation-and-abuse-in-conflict-and-post-conflict-situations.html.

References

Armstrong, K. (2011). *Peace Week Tele-Summit Keynote Speech*. September 18.

Beker, M. (2004). *Screenwriting with a Conscience: Ethics for screenwriters*. Mahwah, NJ: Lawrence Erlbaum Associates.

Brennan Center for Justice at NYU School of Law (2006). Citizens without proof: A survey of American's possession of documentary proof of citizenship and photo identification, www.brennancenter.org.

Cody, D. (2007). *Juno. The Shooting Script*. New York: Newmarket Press.

Dalai Lama, The (2011). *How to be Compassionate*. New York: Atria Books.

Ebert, R. (1991). Oliver Stone defends JFK against conspiracy of dunces, *Chicago Sun Times*, December 22.

Eliot, T.S. (1961). Burnt Norton. In Mack, Dean and Frost (Eds.). *Modern Poetry*. New York: Prentice Hall.

Field, S. (2005). *Screenplay: The foundations of screenwriting* (revised). New York: Bantam Dell.

Finnegan, M. (2007). *Newshour Extra*. www.pbs.org, June 26.

Gardner, E. (2011). Judge may allow war veteran's bombshell lawsuit against 'Hurt Locker' to continue. *Hollywood Reporter*, August 9.

Gates, B. (2011). *Annual Letter from the Bill and Melinda Gates Foundation*.

Giri, Swami Sri Yukteswar (1990). *The Holy Science*. Self-realization Fellowship, Los Angeles, CA.

Gould, S.J., Gupta, P.B. & Grabner-Krauter, S. (1997). Product placement in movies, *Journal of Current Issues and Research in Advertising, 19*(1): 37–50.

Guttmacher Institute (2011). Facts on induced abortion in the U.S. See www.guttmacher.org.

Harris, M. (2010). Inventing Facebook, *New York Magazine*, September 17.

Karniouchina, E.V., Uslay, C. & Erenburg, G. (2011). Do marketing media have life cycles? The case of product placement in movies, *Journal of Marketing, 75*, 27–48.

Kennedy, R.F. (1993). *Collected Speeches*. New York: Viking Penguin.

King, M.L. Jr. (2007). *Conscience for Change. The lost Massey lectures.* Toronto: House of Anansi Press.

King, M.L. Jr. (1968). *I Have a Dream*. New York: Grosset and Dunlap.

Leadingham, C., Moschella, J.E. & Vartanian, H.M. (Eds.). (1992). *Peace prayers*. San Francisco: Harper Collins.

Leifermann, H.P. (1975). *Crystal Lee. A woman of inheritance.* New York: Macmillan.

Mallac, G. de. (1989). *Gandhi's Seven Steps to Global Change.* Santa Fe, NM: Ocean Tree Books.

Marcuse, H. (2007). *Art and Liberation. Collected papers, vol. 4.* London/New York: Routledge.

Mata, Sri Daya (1999). *A World in Transition.* Self-realization Fellowship, Los Angeles, CA.

Moon, Ban Ki. Secretary General of the United Nations. Letter to Larysa Kondracki, August 11, 2011.

Muggeridge, M. (1971). *Something Beautiful for God. Mother Teresa of Calcutta.* London: William Collins Sons and Co Ltd.

New York Times. (1996). Philadephia makers settle suit, March 20.

——. (2011). Directing trust is far from friends, March 27.

NRC.GOV. (2002). *Backgrounder, Three Mile Island Accident,* U.S. NRC, Office of Public Affairs.

Orwell, G. (2002). *Essays*. New York: Alfred A. Knopf.

Simmons, A.M. (2011). Ex-skinhead seen as stereotype victim by his black lawyer. *Los Angeles Times*, August 1.

The American Heritage Dictionary. (2006). Boston/New York: Houghton Mifflin Company.

The Holy Bible. King James Version (1998). Grand Rapids, MI: World Publishing.

Tutu, D. (2004). *God Has a Dream*. New York: Doubleday.

Weiner, J. (2011). David Schwimmer: Directing 'Trust' is far from *Friends. The New York Times*, March 25.

www.dosomething.org/tipsandtools/11-facts-about-music-education.

Yogananda, P. (1996). *Spiritual Diary.* Self-realization Fellowship, Los Angeles, CA.

Index